TRAINING
IS
BITTER

REFLECTIONS
ON LIFE,
EFFORT, AND
ACROBATICS
WITH MASTER
TRAINER LU YI

LU YI

WITH DEVIN HOLT

TRAINING IS BITTER
Copyright © 2023 Devin Holt

Published by
Periodgraph Press
www.periodgraph.com

ISBN (paperback): 979-8-9872189-0-7

Book design by Domini Dragoone, www.DominiDragoone.com
Cover image: © Terry Lorant. Lu Yi spots Lorenzo Pisoni in a handstand, 1990
Author photo: © Eric Gillet

DISCLAIMERS

This is a book about acrobatics. As such, it offers occasional explanations of acrobatic techniques and their creative uses from a master of the art form. Do not confuse these explanations with acrobatic instruction, which they are not. Do not attempt to learn acrobatics from the descriptions, pictures, or stories in this book, which could lead to injury. Do not, as the saying goes, try this at home. An experienced, professional coach is an essential element of acrobatic training.

Also, this book is a memoir based on dictated interviews translated from Mandarin to English, with supplemental research including books, photos, show programs, documentary footage, and other sources. The recreated scenes, dialogue, narrative, and anecdotes are subject to the fallible nature of memory and the challenges of translation.

CONTENTS

A famous Peking opera actor described
basic training as six steps, all sweat!

First sweat from skin,
Second sweat from muscles,
Third sweat from ligaments,
Fourth sweat from bones,
Fifth sweat from behind the knees,
Sixth sweat from blood.

— MASTER TRAINER LU YI,
quoted in the program for the final performance of
The Nanjing Project, a three-month series of acrobatic
workshops conducted by the Nanjing Acrobatic
Troupe in New South Wales, Australia, in 1984.

ACT ONE

PREVIOUS PAGE: Zhang Jian Guo performs as the top and Lu Yi as the base in "Picking Flowers on Top of a Head," a trick Lu Yi invented while working with the Nanjing Acrobatic Troupe, circa 1973. Photo: Nanjing Acrobatic Troupe/Lu Yi Family Collection.

ONE

THE GREAT WORLD

I often tell people that I have accomplished four things in my life. First, I improved circus in Nanjing, China, until it was quite outstanding. When I arrived in Nanjing as a young performer in the 1950s, the Nanjing Acrobatic Troupe was brand-new. By the time I left, it was one of the top acrobatic troupes in China. As artistic director, I created several new tricks and improved many others, while creating and implementing safe, effective methods of acrobatic training.

Next, I took Chinese circus to Australia. In the 1980s, the Nanjing Acrobatic Troupe traveled there for a performance tour, and returned the following year to teach students from all over the country in a program sponsored by the Australian government. It was the first Chinese Acrobatics training program in the country. The prime minister came to our end-of-session performance.

The third thing, you may already know: I brought Chinese circus to the United States. I first came here when the Nanjing Acrobatic Troupe performed with the Big Apple Circus in 1988.

3

Later, I moved to Berkeley and taught acrobatics to the Pickle Family Circus, and then to students at the San Francisco School of Circus Arts, where I became artistic director. Many of my students went on to successful careers, performing at prestigious festivals and in well-regarded companies such as Cirque du Soleil, 7 Fingers, Cirque Éloize, and others. The school is still there and is called Circus Center now.

Lastly, I took American circus, of a certain kind, to China. Working with the Circus Center's Clown Conservatory, we took American clowns trained in the school's methods to China for cross-cultural performances and workshops.

Those are the four things I have done. They were not easy. Some took a great amount of effort.

Effort frequently becomes the most important element in success. A person may be born talented but lazy; someone like that is easy to dissuade—push them and they fall over. But a determined person is different. Try to hold them back, and they slip through your arms toward the goal. Here is a Chinese phrase, one I used to teach all of my young American students: Qín xué kǔ liàn. It means to study diligently, to train assiduously. Americans might say it's something like putting in blood, sweat, and tears. I used to line my students up and have them shout that phrase at the beginning of class: "Qín xué kǔ liàn!" I did this because I wanted the young people in my Youth Circus program to remember that building great skills requires great effort. I wanted them to remember that training is difficult. I wanted them to remember that training is bitter.

It takes a certain kind of person to push through the rigor of acrobatic training. You need a sincere desire to accomplish the tricks. Where that desire comes from is different for each person. Mine came from a deep, immediate love of the acrobatic art form. Some people are motivated by fame and attention, others by money, or the simple need to survive. Lots of people might find motivation from a combination of all those things. Regardless, in each of these hypothetical persons' lives, there will be a moment when they recognize their own strength of will. A moment when they feel the need to push past all the obstacles and grab what they want with both hands. For me, that moment came when I was about ten years old, and a man stomped on my fingers. I have never forgotten him, or the way he treated me—as if I didn't even matter, simply because I was poor.

This incident happened inside a place called Dashijie, around 1949. Dashijie, which translates roughly as "Great World" in English, was an entertainment center in Shanghai and a popular place for circus shows in the forties and fifties. I've seen bigger, better places since. But, as a kid, Dashijie struck me as a magnificent, exciting entertainment palace. Its five floors of attractions seemed to have everything: Beijing opera; Shanghai opera; magic shows; cross-talk comedy shows; Chinese and foreign films; gambling; noodles and rice buns for sale; a rooftop space for food and drinks. It opened at noon and closed around ten o'clock at night. Buy one ticket, and you can watch as much as you want, as long as you want. A real bargain. People came early and stayed late, sometimes bringing their own food and drinks.

The floors had various stages, with smaller shows on the side, and the larger, higher-quality ones in the center. I watched some of everything, but it was on a center stage that I witnessed the performance style that would change my life—zá jì, or "acrobatic shows." Those were always in the center. I stared with a mix of fascination and envy. I loved the circus right away.

On my initial trips to Dashijie, I could not linger too long. I had not come looking for entertainment. I had come looking for cigarette butts. That was my job. It was not a job where I was on the clock, it was more like an independent enterprise. An enterprise for poor street people with no other options.

I started scavenging cigarettes soon after my family came to Shanghai from Yancheng, in Jiangsu Province, about three hundred kilometers to the north. I don't remember much about Yancheng, beyond a small rural area, and me playing outdoors or swimming in the river. My parents, Lu Guo Cai and Wu A'Si, were farmers, and my grandfather worked as a receptionist in a small, local government office. The boat that took us along the Yangtze River to Shanghai was small, crowded, and frightening. It had no cover, only a sail, and carried about twenty families, which was clearly more than it was meant to hold. The boat people who paddled us warned everyone to keep still for safety. Before we left, they told us to burn incense and pray to the gods, also for safety. I did both.

My parents said little about the move to Shanghai. I knew there was not enough food, not enough harvest, and thought maybe it had something to do with a natural disaster. We went to the city to try and make a better living. Lots of people did that at the time. I offered no resistance or opinion; I just followed my parents.

We had nowhere to stay, so my parents gathered up some plywood and took it to a slum in Huangpu District. There, they assembled a small house on the street, about the size of a shed. In the winter, we all slept close together to keep warm. In the summer, sometimes we slept outside to stay cool. We used a tiny, portable charcoal stove to cook, mostly outside, but in the house if it rained. On a good day, we might have lard to add to the noodles for flavor (and for protein). Most of the time, we did not. Sometimes, when the winters got very cold, we brought the stove inside and used it for heat.

When you live this way, it's important to contribute to the family. It's not like America, where the parents work and the kids focus on school or play. When you're very, very poor, everyone has to help. That's how I started selling cigarettes. My brother and I would gather the butts from the street, and our father helped us sell them. My mother washed clothes for a variety of families around Shanghai. She had the reputation of someone who does a good job.

In those days, I used my given name, Lu Shun Yin. My elder brother was called Lu Shun Jin. My two younger sisters were Lu Yue Zhen and Lu Gui Ying, and I had another older brother who left our family to live with my father's sister before I was born. My name and my brother's name represented our family's aspirations. My name had the Chinese word for silver, my brother's the word for gold. Both our names used the word "smoothly," as in, without problems or obstacles. If these names were supposed to help us easily find silver, gold, or prosperity, they did not. At least, not back then. We left Yancheng as poor farmers and arrived in Shanghai as poor street people. But who knows? Maybe those names helped us find cigarette butts.

I would wander the streets until I had a good clump of discarded cigarettes. These I would twist apart one by one, until the small bits of leftover, unsmoked tobacco formed a decent pile. That tobacco got rerolled, then sold on the streets to people who couldn't afford regular cigarettes. It wasn't exactly turning trash into treasure, but it did turn something people threw out into money for the family.

My cigarette wanderings took me around Huangpu and other places, but I found myself drawn to Dashijie. With so many people there, it made a good market. And, because people smoked inside in those days, it was a good place to find cigarette butts. It didn't hurt that I wanted to watch all the shows too. My favorite back then was Beijing opera. Sometimes, I would get a broom and swing it around, pretending it was a sword on the stage. I imitated the kicks and dances of opera and the wild tricks of the acrobatic shows. I played around with cartwheels and my best attempts at flips. I tried to mimic the moves on that center stage: boys who flipped and folded through hoops; girls who bent their backs into impossible contortions; gymnastic tumblers; pole climbers; hand balancers. I had fun pretending to be in the circus. It brought me some rare, precious moments of joy in an otherwise difficult time.

I worked the crowds at the shows too. I would get down on my knees and crawl around to find the fattest cigarette butts. Some people did not like that. They would spit or give me mean looks. One of those people was the man I talked about earlier. I reached near his leg to grab a cigarette, and suddenly his foot came down on my fingers. Pain shot through my hand and up my arm. The man did not move or apologize. He just leered at me.

"Hey, you idiot," he said, scoffing. "Homeless kid."

I hated how he acted. *He should show more respect*, I thought. It's true that I was young and I was poor. But he did not need to do that. I told myself I would never be mean like him. I would never treat someone as if they did not matter at all; as if they could just be brushed aside, like leftover cartons on the sidewalk. I've tried to live out that promise my whole career. I try to do so even now. At the same time, his disrespect made me want to become a person worth greater respect. The kind of person who does not have to crawl around on the floor, where it's easy for mean people to stomp on your fingers. Of course, I had no idea how to make that transformation at ten years old. But I could not let people like him chase me away from Dashijie. Giving up is not an option when you're poor.

I needed the crowds for the cigarette business, and the crowds went to Dashijie, so I did too. But there was more to it than the cigarette business. Somewhere, deep inside, I sensed that the things happening on those stages would be important to my life. And, sure enough, thanks to my time at Dashijie, I did get to learn those tricks that inspired me.

Was it worth getting my fingers stomped on by a mean smoker? I guess I can't say no—because I was in for much worse once I started training.

TWO

NO PARENT,
NO GUARDIAN,
NO AUDITION

On the day I first met him, Pan Yin sat at a small table in the corner of his acrobatic troupe's training space at Dashijie. A stocky, muscular man of medium height with a lot of facial hair, Pan Yin came from a circus family and had played a soldier in Beijing opera, a role that requires heavy makeup and lots of acrobatics. He still carried himself with a bit of that military attitude. He did not speak much or appear to take any particular interest in me. I stared around the room at the people stretching, tumbling, practicing handstands and other tricks.

I had been encouraged to meet Pan Yin by an older man at Dashijie named Chen Jing Tai. He noticed me one day when I was playing around with a stick, pretending it was a sword in a Chinese opera. Chen Jing Tai was tall, with an honest face. He didn't say anything to me at first, but he must have thought my pretend moves and untrained cartwheels looked okay, or less than terrible, because he started letting me into Dashijie for free. Chen Jing Tai happened to work for Pan Yin's wife, and knew that Pan Yin was branching out on his own after working with his father, who ran the Pan Family Youth Acrobatics Troupe. Chen Jing Tai made the introductions and told me where to find the trainer. I went alone; no parents, no guardian, no siblings.

After we introduced ourselves, Pan Yin asked if I wanted to apprentice for the circus. I told him I did, and he nodded. There was no audition, no demonstration of skills. Pan Yin simply handed me a paper with a list of terms. It covered a lot of things, which I probably should have thought about carefully: That I would become an apprentice, but my family would remain entirely responsible for me. I would get no food, no pay, no medical help, nothing. There was no guarantee I would perform. Pan Yin's only obligation was to teach me acrobatics; for that, I had to help the troupe however I was asked. The term was for five years.

Of course, I did not think about any of this stuff carefully. I was only a boy, with no schooling or lessons of any kind. I could hardly read the characters on the paper, much less negotiate based on what they listed. I signed and gave the paper back to Pan Yin. And just like that, I became an apprentice member of the Eagle Sphere Acrobatics Troupe, which soon changed its name to the Red Acrobatic Troupe—a name that fit the times better after the Communist Party took power in 1949.

The first day of training went pretty well. Everything felt fresh, like the moment right before the sun comes out. Pan Yin didn't have anyone else teaching at that time. There was no "welcome to the team" event or anything. I just fell in with the others, doing my best to imitate the movements. But that was okay. Most of the other students were younger than me and not so advanced. And I was excited to be there, to finally learn these tricks I had admired from afar. It seemed like I had found something with a better future than picking up cigarette butts.

That part was true. But I would not stay quite so excited for long.

THREE

A BITTER FAMILY

Chinese Acrobatics has a similar culture to martial arts. The school is like a family, and your fellow apprentices become your siblings—but your position in the troupe hierarchy is decided by when you joined, not your age. So training partners who joined before me are considered seniors within the group, even if I'm older. In my generation I was the third member, relatively high up, because I joined when Pan Yin was still starting the company. The performers I had been watching at Dashijie were mostly older, closer to my father's generation. Several of the people from Pan Yin's troupe went on to long careers in acrobatics, working with me all over the world: Yang Xiao Di, who joined us on our Big Apple Circus tour, became a clown and eventually moved to New York; Yin Guo Gang and Yin Guo Ming, a pair of brothers who made a comedy act by making all sorts of amusing sounds with their mouths, like bird noises and music; and most importantly, Xia Ke Min, who joined years after I did but became my lifelong training partner and closest friend.

Training with Pan Yin started early in the morning and ended late at night. Twelve-hour days were common. Our training space was sometimes on the first and sometimes on the third floor. We focused mostly on four things: handstands, somersaults, leg stretches, and backbends—a backbend is when a person stands up and bends backward from the hips. It's an important part of tumbling and contortion. We worked on all of those moves over and over, mastering the basics until they became as simple as breathing. That's how Chinese Acrobatics works. You create a foundation of basics, and build everything from there.

A common Chinese Acrobatics warm-up includes a series of kicks: front kick; side kick; circle kick to the left; circle kick to the right; back kick; spinning kick; spinning kick with a jump; maybe a butterfly kick or butterfly kick with a twist in the middle, if you have the skill level. After each kick we took a step forward, then executed the next kick, all in a line, moving back and forth across the room to a slow, hand-clapped rhythm from the coach or a fellow student. Under Pan Yin, we trained on solid floors with no mats. Dive rolls, back handsprings, round-off back tucks: I practiced them all on cold, hard concrete. There was no heating in the winter, no air-conditioning in the summer. But we knew better than to complain. Most acrobatic apprentices, like me, came from poor families. For people like us, it's better to just keep going. Whatever the temperature, whatever the circumstances, you have to get used to it.

Sometimes Pan Yin even used the weather against us. We learned to spin plates while standing out in the cold for hours. To spin a plate on the end of a stick, you need to make a small, circular movement with your wrist. Pan Yin believed that if you could make that movement outside in harsh, difficult weather, it would be that much easier indoors. My hands ached for hours and hours after that; the cold seeping into my bones, as if ice had melted inside my veins.

Handstands we learned against a wall at first, then—once you could balance—on the open floor. The handstand is the base movement for all Chinese Acrobatics. Nothing is more important. This was true in my early days training with Pan Yin, and remained true as I became a coach in China, Australia, and the U.S. It is still true today. If you go to an acrobatics class at the San Francisco Circus Center right now, they will most likely start teaching you handstands on the first day. And you will learn them against the wall, same as I did.

The reason people practice handstands against the wall is simple: balance. Balancing without a wall or a person to spot you is almost impossible at first. The wall handstand works like this: Start by facing the wall, two or three feet away. Bend over and put your hands on the floor, a few inches out from the wall. You should have one foot close to your hands and one foot farther back, like a runner setting up for a race. Now kick, starting with the back leg, up and toward the wall until your center of gravity is straight above your hands. Get as close to the wall as possible, walking your hands toward it if you can, letting your feet touch the wall to help you balance.

Once you get into position, it's important to focus on the shoulder. The shoulder must push up, like it wants to come out of the joint. It should feel like reaching for a high ceiling while holding a weight. Squeeze the ground with your fingers. That part is also important. When you squeeze the floor, it distributes the weight toward the top of your palm and onto your fingers, instead of onto your wrists. By squeezing, your fingers create ten little pads to keep you balanced in the correct spot. This is much easier on a flat, solid floor, so don't practice on a squishy mat.

In the handstand, your body should be tight, but not tense. You want to engage the muscles in your stomach, back, and butt; but without engaging them so much that you can't make adjustments. We have a Mandarin word: fàngsōng. Relaxed, but not floppy. Not like a banana. Also, point the toes—no lazy feet.

Of course these steps are outlined for information only. I have to warn you not to practice any of this without proper instruction. Acrobatics is not something you can learn from a book.

Under Pan Yin, the minimum time for a serious person to hold a handstand was twenty minutes; better if you could do thirty. Sometimes we held them much longer. Maybe even an hour. Pan Yin wandered the floor and delivered corrections, usually with a hard stick. He would yell a command, then slap the offending body part.

"Push shoulder"—thwack! "Point toe"—thwack! "Straighten leg"—thwack!

If your technique did not improve, you could expect a beating. Pan Yin used to hit us every day, sometimes every hour. He would beat us for mistakes and, other times, beat us for no apparent reason; even when everyone seemed to be working very hard and doing well. We spent our days terrified that the teacher would hit us at any moment. This is a very dangerous way to train. You get so nervous thinking about that stick that it's easy to mess up. You're so scared, maybe you start shaking a little and you jump wrong or land wrong. It's very easy to hurt yourself in that situation, when you're terrified the teacher might beat you to death. It made training very bitter. Very sad. Effort and discipline should never come from fear. But that's not how Pan Yin saw it. In his world, the troupe needed people to listen and to learn fast. The stick and the fist made that happen.

One of the worst parts of our early training was the stretching. You need flexible legs and a flexible back for acrobatics. Pan Yin used horrible methods to make us flexible quickly. He would push our legs into deep splits, or pull them sideways past our heads. We would yell, cry out, cry real tears; Pan Yin did not care. He only cared about the flexibility. I especially hated how he stretched the young girls for contortion acts. I could live with my own pain, but watching other people suffer, I got so mad.

Contortion requires a very flexible upper back—that part where your back, neck, and shoulders all come together. It was considered a girl's act in those days. Pan Yin would shove his foot into a young girl's back, then pull her arms toward him as far as possible. He would do this over and over, sometimes using other people to help pull the girl's arms. They would yell and cry in pain; Pan Yin would beat them, just like the boys. I hated Pan Yin for that. I hated him so much.

Although everyone was hit by the coaches, some were hit more than others, and I was one of them. Pan Yin used me as an example. As the third person of my generation, I had a high enough rank that other students would get scared if they saw me get a beating. But I didn't have such a high status that a beating might cause trouble for the troupe. The first and second apprentices at Red Acrobatic Troupe were better protected. The first apprentice's family was close to Pan Yin, and Pan Yin knew he could not beat the child of a friend very often. The second apprentice's mother sold dumplings in Dashijie. She came by often with dumplings for the teacher. But people saw me as a lowly, no-money street kid—only the son of migrant workers—with no one to advocate for him. They could beat me and get away with it.

The bruises used to make me feel ashamed. In public shower rooms, I would cover myself with a towel to hide them. I didn't want people to think I was a bad child; someone so reckless and disloyal that his parents beat him. Of course, today people would see those beatings differently. No one would say it's my fault I got hit by Pan Yin. If you ran a circus like that now, you would go to jail. People would call it child abuse. They would say it's wrong to hit kids, no matter what. It was wrong back then too. I just couldn't do anything about it.

Sometimes, people ask why I endured such harsh methods. Why didn't I leave? It's simple. I loved the circus. I loved acrobatics. I wanted to learn those tricks. And I felt a strong sense of pride that I could accomplish such fantastic physical feats. Early in my career, I beamed when I started to get paid—five yuan per show, a pittance today, but more than most troupe members my age got at the time. That thrilled me. I believed strongly in the idea of pushing through. Here's one more Chinese phrase: nǔ lì. It means, roughly, to put forth a great effort. I wanted to prove that I could achieve mastery and earn respect through hard, consistent work. Anytime I wanted to give up, I had the image of that man who stomped on my fingers to motivate me. If I kept training, I could show him, and everyone, that I was not just some "homeless kid."

Also, I was young. Very young and very poor. People with empty stomachs sometimes have the best endurance.

When people ask me about those days, I often recommend a film: 1993's *Farewell, My Concubine*. It follows two lifelong friends who train for Beijing opera, and shows some harsh training methods like the ones I endured. It's not exactly the same; just close enough to give you an idea. Another thing I do is let them feel my head. I will take the person's hand and guide it up, a few inches past my forehead, where they can feel the clump of scar tissue, permanent bumps left on my head by Pan Yin's stick. That's proof of what I went through.

However, the Pan Yin beating that stands out the most did not happen to me. That one happened to Xia Ke Min. But you could say it affected us both.

FOUR

'WHAT HAPPENED TO YOUR FACE?'

The worst of the Pan Yin trouble for Xia Ke Min happened outside of town.

The stages at Dashijie rotated performers, so sometimes Pan Yin booked us for another show somewhere else. A common destination was Big Star Company, a center with the same concept as Dashijie but smaller, with fewer attractions. We traveled in small, three-legged taxi cars that were popular with fishermen. The cars were only supposed to fit three people, but we were limber circus kids and would cram in as many as five. We rolled through the bicycle-crowded streets with hoops, plates, bike parts, and all kinds of circus equipment hugged tight to our bodies—and spilling out every which way from those little cars. Xia still gets a laugh thinking about our circus troupe heading down Nanjing Road like that.

Xia always had a great sense of humor and liked to play. He enjoyed Dashijie even more than me. Ask him about those days, and you might hear this old Shanghai saying: "If you went to Shanghai and you didn't visit Dashijie, then you can't say you've been to Shanghai." Xia's favorite attraction there was the same as mine, Beijing opera. Then it was movies and the sillier stuff, like the room filled with trick mirrors. Anytime Xia could slip away, he was likely to sneak into a film—monster pictures were a favorite—or while away his time in front of mirrors that made him appear tall, fat, misshapen, or just generally strange.

This sense of playfulness served Xia well as a performer, especially after he got too old for high-level acrobatics. But it made his training years more difficult. The tiniest joke could incur the wrath of Pan Yin. That may be why Xia never found the same level of enthusiasm for circus as I did. Everyone knows I remember our training as "bitter." Xia was more likely to recall it as "torture."

Xia came from an artistic family. His father played drums for opera companies and his mother danced for them. Both performed regularly at Dashijie, so apprenticing their eldest boy to Pan Yin's circus made perfect sense. They knew the trainer, the performance circuit, and the financial realities of the time. The acrobatic troupe offered a way to keep him in the family business. Xia's father dropped him off in the Dashijie training space early in the morning. Xia did not want to stay, often running after his father as he walked away. Pan Yin would scoop the boy up to hold him back.

Xia joined a handful of years after me, around 1955. He was born in 1948, which made him younger, and smaller, than most other members of the troupe. Because of this, he made a good "top" for partner acrobatics. That's how we ended up working together. With a lighter person on top, you can make some partner tricks quickly. The bottom person, or "base," does most of the balancing from underneath, so the top only has to hold themselves straight and tight, as if they were a heavy broomstick. They don't have to have a perfect handstand.

I liked Xia right away. He was quick, smart, talented, funny, and, despite his age, already had performance experience. Xia's parents had put him in shows as a dancer, or to play a child, or, once, in a role where he dressed up like a very old man. I also felt a sense of responsibility to Xia. I was older and had been in the troupe longer. That made me an elder circus brother. I needed to look out for him, and help his development however I could. If the circus was a family, we were an elder brother and younger brother who stuck together. But I was only a boy. I could not protect him from the leader of the troupe.

On the day Pan Yin delivered his worst beating, the troupe went to Suzhou, about a hundred kilometers west of Shanghai. Everyone unloaded the gear and started practice as per normal. Xia ran through some of his partner tricks with Pan Yin, but could not hold his handstand perfectly straight, and had a little trouble balancing. Things soon turned ugly.

When Xia tried to jump into a handstand on top of Pan Yin's hands, his weight went too far forward. Pan Yin had to turn and hold Xia's hands until his feet hit the ground. On another try, Xia didn't jump high enough for Pan Yin to get under him. Xia fell back to the ground before they even reached a handstand. Pan Yin was not pleased. Xia tried again with a better jump, but still did not get his weight in the correct place. Pan Yin, disgusted, dropped him. He turned his back and let Xia fall from midair to the ground.

After Xia landed, Pan Yin turned back and kicked him. He kicked him again and again.

Then he hit Xia's face. And hit it again. Pan Yin continued to beat Xia—even longer than his normal, cruel standard. He beat him for so long that Pan Yin's wife finally intervened.

"You can't hit kids like that," she called out. "They're too small."

Pan Yin stopped. Xia slinked away, his face painful, swollen, and puffy. When show time arrived, Xia was not excused. He still had to perform. The other troupe members gathered around him before he went onstage, pointing and asking questions.

"What happened to your face? What happened to your face?" they said, one after the other.

Xia did not perform any doubles tricks that night. Instead, he served as the finale for the trick bicycle act, where many people climb onto a bike as it goes around the stage. In China, this trick is called "Peacock Displaying Its Feathers" and is attributed to a postal workers' circus group. Xia was the last person to climb atop the pile of acrobats as the bike whirled around the stage—a common role for the smallest troupe member. Xia raised his hands and forced a smile onto his swollen, puffy face. That was the life of a young circus acrobat. Smiling through pain.

Soon after this incident, Xia left Pan Yin's circus. His parents, shocked at the severity of his treatment, did not force him to return. They saw the marks on his face, how much he hurt. I saw it too. As with the harsh stretching techniques used on the young girls, this made me hate our trainer even more. I accepted my own bitter circumstances; but I could not stand to see them pushed on others. Also, I missed Xia. He had been my younger circus brother, and now Pan Yin's cruelty had forced him away.

This is not the right way, I thought. Training should be bitter because what you are trying to do is difficult, not because of your treatment. But there was nothing I could do to change the circus or to bring Xia back. Not yet.

FIVE

'SHOW THEM WE ARE STRONG'

As bitter as training was, it did have some good results. By my mid-teens, in 1956, I was standing on a stage in Beijing with Premier Zhou Enlai.

"Now, you are representing China," he told our troupe. "You have to show them that we are strong and powerful."

In China, the premier is an important, high-ranking government position. Zhou Enlai's visit came at the end of our last rehearsal in Beijing, on the eve of my first trip overseas. I had been one of the people selected for an all-Shanghai troupe, among the best performers from our city. Zhou Enlai's arrival came as a complete surprise and a great honor. We were already impressed to be in the capital; to have a high-level official address us was especially thrilling. We didn't even know he was there during rehearsal. After we finished running the show, our stage manager came out and told us to stay put, that

Premier Zhou would meet us on the stage. It was a once-in-a-lifetime moment. I'll never forget it.

Zhou Enlai told us how people used to think of China as a sickly place, the weakest country in East Asia. But our upcoming performances would help restore the reputation and honor of our country. This idea filled me with pride. A young man born in a small, poor village and raised on the streets of Shanghai, now representing China to the world. It felt like a true accomplishment. Zhou Enlai must have been pretty impressed with us too, because, after that meeting, the troupe started to get special treatment, like better, more sophisticated food instead of simple buns.

The tour took us to Europe, through the Eastern Bloc countries that were associated with the Soviet Union. That kind of political affiliation fit with the ideals of the Chinese government. Those of us in the troupe hardly thought about the political aspect though. Or, at least, I didn't. I was just thrilled to travel, to represent our country, and to meet a new audience in every new place. It helped that the audiences were thrilled to meet us too. People treated us like stars. Every night they cheered, every night they brought us flowers and love. Those were some of the best times of my life.

The shows on that tour started with an energetic number that brought most of the troupe on stage. Acrobats running, tumbling, doing martial arts kicks. A very happening, busy number to get the audience excited. It's not focused so much on any one person or group; it's almost like a preview that gives the crowd an idea of how much the acrobats can do. An intriguing, chaotic array to get them leaning forward in their seats. You might see five, six, ten, people all running and tumbling in different directions—but they won't do their best tricks yet. If there's a hoop diving act coming later, someone might set up a hoop very quickly, hop through, and take it back down, while others tumble around them in a circle. The juggler might run across the stage with their clubs while doing the simple cascade pattern or a very high toss. In America, people call this a charivari. It's a very traditional opening number used in shows around the world. If you go to a circus tomorrow, you will probably see a charivari in the beginning.

In general, circus shows have four highlight moments. The opener that we just talked about, to get the crowd into it. Then again at the end of the first half, right before intermission, to give the audience something to talk about—and to make sure they come back. You need another highlight for the opening of the second half, and a big, exciting number at the end. Think "grand finale." Acts with more people and big, physical acrobatic skills make the best highlights. Hoop diving could be a good way to end the first half. The trick bicycle act, the one where the whole cast climbs onto the bike and rides around, might make for an excellent grand finale. Or you could reverse them. But you probably would not end the show with a solo or duo act.

That's not an insult. There are many great acts with only one or two people: A hand balancer who stacks chairs until they're twenty feet high then pushes up into a one-arm handstand. A pair of pole climbers who go halfway up and push their legs out straight, like human flags. Some of the most talented jugglers work alone. All of these acts can impress an audience, and fit well in the middle of a show. But you generally want to end with a group number because of the higher energy level. When lots of people come on stage for a tall pyramid or acrobatic lion dance, it creates a sense of collective excitement. And the audience responds to that excitement.

For the European shows, we always had the opening charivari but varied the other acts. It depended on the audience, the space, and the mood and ideas of the directors. I had little say in what went where in those days. For the trick bicycle, the greatest number of people who climbed on in that tour was around ten. This is somewhat low-level by the standards I set later in Nanjing (we got the number up to twenty-six), but the crowds didn't mind. You can tell how an audience feels during a show, and those audiences loved us. Also, there were parties every night. That made it pretty clear.

The parties were grand affairs, with lots of food and drinks. The food I found a little difficult to enjoy. I don't mean it was bad. This was good stuff—lots of meat and wine—it's just that Western food tasted a little odd to me at first. And, of course, they served it with Western-style utensils, like forks. Thankfully, the tour managers taught us how to use Western utensils before we left. They told us all kinds of things: how to behave, how to dance, not to drink too much alcohol. They even gave us papers with written rules and reminders. They obviously didn't want any embarrassments. We had to remember that we were representing China at all times. Thanks to those lessons, the parties never felt awkward. I knew what to expect, even if it was different.

Well, I guess dancing was a bit awkward. I could only dance a little, and just simple steps, following people.

Drinking could lead to trouble though. Our official guidance on the paper said the best scenario would be to only drink "one third of the cup." So if someone hands you a glass, you sip a third and quietly get rid of the rest. I didn't always follow that, and neither did the others. It was easy to have a bit extra when the show went well. In Romania, a juggler got so drunk they had to take him out of the party. That guy seemed kind of troublesome. He was always trying to get into relationships, like dating relationships, with people in the cities we visited. In Romania, I think he did do some dating.

The tour ended in Budapest, the capital of Hungary. The Hungarians liked our show so much they asked us to stay longer, and without another stop to get to, the troupe leaders accepted. We agreed to stay in Budapest for ten more days. But those ten days turned out to be quite frightening. A troupe focused on performance was about to get a front-row seat to a revolution.

SIX

A REVOLUTION OUTSIDE
THE WINDOW

O n the first day of the incident in Budapest, people came into the hotel with guns. This was a nice hotel, right in central Budapest with a view of the Városliget, the main city park. The intruders all seemed to have big mustaches, and looked more like regular people than soldiers. I guessed they were the anti-government side. They didn't hurt any of the acrobats, and as far as I know didn't even threaten us. But the Chinese consulate and the troupe leaders told us to stay put. Wait in our rooms, sit still. No performance, no parties, nothing. Something had come to the capital. Nothing to do but wait.

The Hungarian Revolution was an uprising against the Soviet Union's domination of Hungary. Many people, especially young people, didn't want to live under the Soviets anymore, and the Soviet government responded with military force. That's the very short version. I didn't know much about the details of the Hungarian Revolution in 1956 and I still don't today. If you want to learn about that, you'll have to get a different book. People with guns had occupied our hotel. And we couldn't leave. That's the important part.

On the second day, we heard gunshots outside. Not all at once or all the time. More like one shot here, one shot there. We sat in our rooms, hiding from everything—the chaos outside, the guns in the lobby. On the following day, the Russian government sent tanks to protect the hotel. I peered out the window, watching as people filled the streets and the park. I could tell some people were there to protest against the government, but I could not tell which side was which, or who was who. There were lots of angry people. Later, someone on the roof shot at the protestors. It was a gruesome scene. Very cruel. In the following days, the protestors decided to tear down the huge statue of Stalin on the edge of the Városliget. It took all afternoon and half the night to bring down the monument. Finally, the top section hit the ground with a hard crack. The people celebrated by pounding it to pieces with hammers. *Crack, crack, crack.*

Our troupe started to run out of food. We drank one cup of milk and ate one slice of bread per day. That's how low supplies got. Then the Chinese consulate in Hungary decided we needed to leave. Simple as that, no more waiting; the decision came down from the top. We had no say in it. Not that I wanted to stay in the hotel anymore. It was scary. It seemed like we might be killed.

As relieved as we felt to get out of there, it was sad too. People gathered around our equipment truck and our van as we packed. They waved their tickets for the show, crowded up to us to hold them close to our faces. We could only shake our heads, tell them we were sorry. Some of those Hungarians looked devastated. Others had tears in their eyes. They really needed that show. They needed that sense of joy and wonder you get from watching circus. It's an escape from reality, something that reminds you how much is possible. And you need that the most in times of distress. The light means a lot more from the far end of the tunnel.

Guilt weighed me down. Guilt about leaving, about our group canceling shows. But we had no choice. There's a phrase in English, one you've probably heard: "The show must go on." But that doesn't cover everything. It's very difficult to make art in the middle of a war. Very difficult. Sometimes you have to give up and move on to survive—a lesson I would learn more than once in my life. We took our van and equipment truck to Czechoslovakia, which has since split into two countries, the Czech Republic and Slovakia.

The Chinese government made some kind of deal for us to stay at the Czech president's retreat. This place was super fancy. Like a palace, with all kinds of expensive art and antiques every-where. We got in at night and they were holding a party in our honor. Imagine, fifty worn-out people from a Chinese circus who escaped violence and revolution plopped down in the mid-dle of a high-class, central European party! What a change of scenery. We were relieved, thrilled, exhausted, confused—and hungry. A day or so later, we saw in the newspaper that everyone at the hotel was killed. I wasn't sure if it really happened though. *Maybe it's some kind of propaganda*, I thought. I still don't know what happened there. Regardless, it's a good thing we weren't at the hotel to find out.

The troupe stayed at the president's retreat in Czechoslova-kia for three days and then flew back to Nanjing. I arrived home with a lot to think about: not just my experiences from the tour, but ideas for the future.

SEVEN

'IT'S GOING TO BE DIFFERENT'

No more beatings, and no regrets—you could say we did not miss Shanghai at all. The troupe members found a brand-new life in Nanjing, with medical care, better training facilities, and a good salary. Eventually, I was paid ninety-five yuan per month; an impressive income for someone who started out rolling cigarettes on the street. But I suppose it's not true that I had no regrets at all. In the early days in Nanjing, there was one thing that made me sad—Xia Ke Min was not there. He had left our troupe because of Pan Yin's abuse. Now, Pan Yin was gone, things were better, and Xia Ke Min remained in Shanghai. That did not seem right. I harbored a sense of responsibility toward Xia; he was my younger circus brother, and I missed him dearly. Also, he was a very good top. And you always need a good top in the circus.

The troupe moved to Nanjing around 1957. I knew very little about the details, because acrobats didn't participate in the larger decision-making process. As far as we heard, the Nanjing government approached the Shanghai government about acquiring the troupe. It's possible the national government attached some importance to having an acrobatic troupe in Nanjing, which had been the capital under the Kuomintang government before the Communists took over in 1949. It's been considered an important city through much of Chinese history, so maybe they wanted to make a statement with a signature arts troupe there. Regardless, the two cities came to an agreement, and most of the troupe moved to form the People's Acrobatic Troupe of Nanjing. It later became the Acrobatic Troupe of the City of Nanjing, and then later still—when we started traveling overseas a lot—it was changed to the Acrobatic Troupe of Nanjing China. From here on out, we'll just call it the Nanjing Acrobatic Troupe to keep things simple.

They offered Pan Yin a position, but he didn't want to work with a government circus company. He wanted to stay private, and even tried to convince me to stick with him. *No, thank you.* In Nanjing, I was free of Pan Yin's training stick and cruelty for good. In an official government troupe, there was much more regulation. You could not simply beat people and get away with it. The Chinese government treated the troupe like a valued cultural institution, something to show off to the world, and invested the resources that came with such a view. The Nanjing years turned out to be some of my best.

Nanjing is where I developed my own sense of creativity and style; my first feeling of artistic freedom. Our troupe had trainers for beginners, but the older, more experienced acrobats trained on our own. I took advantage of this arrangement to work on what later became my best-known tricks. Chinese

Acrobatics is very traditional, sometimes too traditional. You practice the same thing over and over and over until it is perfect. In Nanjing, I had the flexibility to try things in different ways, and to experiment with many different versions of a trick. This made our shows more exciting, and raised the profile of our troupe. By the time I left, we were considered one of the top three acrobatic companies in China. We performed for high-level government officials and foreign dignitaries often, and were frequently booked abroad. That's why they added "China" as part of the official name of the troupe—we became too good to stay regional. When we went to Switzerland to tour with Circus Knie, for example, the national government wanted to show that we represented the whole country, not just Nanjing.

Nanjing served as my home base as I traveled: back to Europe, to Africa, to Australia, and, eventually, to the U.S. Nanjing is where I shifted my focus from performing to teaching and overall circus development for our troupe—and then for all of China. In the mid-seventies, at age thirty-four, I was selected to lead the Nanjing Acrobatic Troupe, the youngest person to take on the role. I later became vice-chairman of the All-China Association of Acrobatic Artists, which represented acrobats all over the country, and chairman of the association's Jiangsu branch. These positions raised my reputation to the point that I was asked to judge competitions and circus festivals. I judged many competitions within China, almost too many to remember, and some of the most prestigious ones in the West: the Monte Carlo International Circus Festival, held in Monaco, and the Festival Mondial du Cirque de Demain, held in Paris, both in the eighties.

Nanjing is where I wrote *On Teeterboard*, a guidebook that laid out proper training protocols for the teeterboard. That came about after I went to see a circus in Anhui Province. I had already been thinking about teeterboard, and how dangerous it is to train. I had seen a lot of accidents around that time. (If you've never seen a teeterboard, it's similar to the playground equipment that Americans call a teeter-totter, or see-saw. It's like that, but wider with a thick, wooden board. An acrobat stands on one end while someone jumps on the other end, sending the acrobat into the air. There are many, many possible variations and combinations.) Recently, someone had jumped on a teeterboard when no one stood on the other end. He broke his knee. That was fresh in my mind as I watched the acrobats in Anhui train. *They need to be more careful*, I thought. *Teeterboard requires better focus.* I started writing down better ways to train, and turned it into a pamphlet for the region. That's another thing that happened in Nanjing: I learned more characters, got better at reading and writing. The government had a campaign to "stamp out illiteracy" and the troupe had some basic tutors.

The notes I laid out in *On Teeterboard* were mostly about procedure and focus. For example:

> *If you're standing on the teeterboard, don't discuss other subjects with people. If someone jumps on the teeter and you're not paying attention, you're going to go flying. You need to know your partner when you train. Before you decide to do a trick, make sure you understand the trick. Know how it works, how much weight to put on the teeterboard. Stick to procedures. The flyer holds their arms straight and slaps their thighs to say "Ready." Keep that signal each time you train, make it clear.*

I wrote about spotting, too. Spotting is when you stand near someone who is tumbling or doing some other trick, and you slap, push, or tap in just the right place to help them land or finish the trick. If they start to fall, you catch them. You need a very good understanding of timing to spot people in acrobatics. It's not something just anyone can do.

The *On Teeterboard* book was distributed around Jiangsu Province, though it was more of an instructional booklet than an official publication. I never saved a copy, but I stuck with those protocols for years. None of my students got seriously injured doing teeterboard—not in China, not in America—because we stayed focused and trained properly. I'm proud of that. Teaching is a great responsibility.

Also in Nanjing, I became somewhat involved in politics. Not maneuvering or that kind of thing. More like a prominent, engaged citizen. I became a member of the Communist Party. After I won the star performer award at the Nanjing Arts Festival, I was invited to become a member of a cultural organization that met directly with the leaders of the city and province. This was an annual meeting held in the Nanjing Great Hall of the People, or People's Meeting Hall. The meeting lasted seven to ten days and was attended by lots of government officials.

The People's Meeting Hall in Nanjing is quite grand. It has two floors, seats around a thousand people, and was built before the more-famous People's Meeting Hall in Beijing. The Kuomintang government used it before the Communists did. Going to the meeting, I felt a great sense of responsibility; a feeling that the well-being of the city rested upon me. I took it very seriously. I spoke about things that I thought would benefit the entire city, not necessarily just the arts: cleaning up public areas, building more public bathrooms, that kind of stuff. I also made suggestions for ways to help the acrobatic troupe, such as better food, or things we needed for training. The issues I brought up did get some attention from the government, even the circus-specific ones.

Nanjing, of course, is also where I met my wife Wang Hong Zhu, and welcomed my two daughters, Lu Yue and Lu Na. Wang Hong Zhu and I were introduced by a relative of mine, a casual matchmaker, who worked at the same factory as Hong Zhu. For dates we went to parks or movies. Hong Zhu's family did not feel it would be good for her to marry someone in the arts. They thought that performers are too flashy, and are more likely to have affairs. Hong Zhu broke up with me for a while, but we started dating again after she asked to borrow a camera for a trip. I was one of the few people she knew who had access to a camera, because of my work with the acrobatic troupe. She could "picture" us together after that.

For me, the most important part was to create a family. I wanted children—but my job involved long hours and lots of travel. I needed to marry someone who could take care of the kids. For the wedding, we had a very simple ceremony, almost like a regular family dinner; we didn't wear special clothes or anything. We married in the earlier part of the Cultural Revolution, so any hint of fancy stuff would have been a bad idea. "The simpler the better" was a good motto at that time, something that would prove even truer in future events. I do remember one thing from the dinner, though—fish. I really like to eat fish.

One more thing that happened in Nanjing: It's where I changed my name. My parents had given me a name related to wealth and riches, but I wanted something that spoke more to perseverance. Something that spoke to my determination to be the best possible acrobat. To how I pushed through hardships to make a better life. That seemed more relevant, more honest. More like myself. So that's how I became Lu Yi. It means, roughly, persistence, or perseverance. Having a goal. To change the name, I had to go to three or four different offices and get a paper signed from my company stating that a name change would not cause problems. Then I had to convince people to call me by the new name. That took about a year. No one really resisted; they just called me my old name out of habit. This was my strategy: When people called out the old name, I pretended not to hear. Eventually, everyone caught on.

But before I could get to all of that, I was worried about something—or someone—else: Xia Ke Min. He had not had a job for a while, and I wanted him to rejoin the acrobatic troupe. Not long after the move, I went to find him, to explain my experience with the new company; to try my best to convince him to join us.

"It's going to be different," I told him. "It's a government job."

I told him about the better pay, better facilities, and the most important thing, better treatment: "There won't be any more beatings."

Thankfully, Xia Ke Min had some level of trust in me and went along. I was so thrilled to see him come to Nanjing. We were like family. At that time, in the early days in Nanjing, the troupe members lived in shared dorms. Xia Ke Min and I slept in the same room, sometimes in the same bed, bunking together, just like real brothers.

EIGHT

PICKING FLOWERS

I came back from my first overseas tour, the trip to Europe, feeling inspired. Inspired to train harder; and to create new tricks. Our tour leader, Zhang Guo Chu, had encouraged us to study other troupes during the tour, which gave me lots of ideas.

Zhang Guo Chu was a great tour director, someone I stayed in touch with for years. He was from Beijing, and had that tall, built look of many people from the north. He gave good, encouraging speeches that stressed the importance of hard work and dedication to representing our country through the excellence of the troupe. But he was also kind. Zhang Guo Chu had no temper; he never scolded people. He recognized that we were young, many of us teenagers, and offered guidance instead.

"You need to learn from the people you're meeting," he told us. "Take advantage of the opportunity."

I made sure to follow his advice.

In Poland, we went to a show with a trick where someone kicked a bowl onto their head. After the troupe settled in Nanjing, I tried to think of ways to improve on the trick I had seen.

So I added a unicycle. Then a taller unicycle. Then more bowls. All of this took a previous idea and built on it to make something that was already difficult even more difficult. A lot of my ideas worked like that; see a trick, push it further. Over the years, from 1957 until I left for the United States in 1990, that became my specialty. Creativity with acrobatic tricks.

Of course, I wasn't the only person who could be creative. Acrobatics is competitive in that way; not so much between individuals but between troupes. Everyone wants to have the latest, the best, the most difficult trick. You can't stop to rest in a competitive environment like that. Stopping is almost like self-destruction. Because of this, I always tried to have something new in my mind. Something to make the troupe stand out. Also, I recognized that acrobats retire early. If I wanted to stick around for a long time, I would need to use my mind—not just my body. I developed a habit of reading the latest books and magazines about circus.

Sometimes, I took a great effort to keep new tricks a secret. When I created the trick "Picking Flowers on Top of a Head," I limited the practice sessions to night hours, rehearsing after most people had gone home. At that time, the Nanjing Acrobatic Troupe had become a bit more famous, which only added more pressure. I had to try and keep us on top, not let us slip down. The last thing I needed was for some other company to see my idea, start working on it, and debut the trick first. To make things even tenser, "Picking Flowers on Top of a Head" took months and months to get right.

The idea came, again, from a previous trick. I had seen acts where people used a backbend to pick a flower from a vase with their teeth. The trick was good, but the performers had to use a table and a chair for the setup. This meant they had to move a lot of equipment around, and it made the transition into and out of the trick rather clunky and awkward. I wanted to take that idea and make it better, smoother, and more impressive. More difficult.

First, I added a person, myself in this case, to the bottom of the trick. On the bottom person's head would be a vase filled with flowers. Also on the vase would be balance points for a Chinese handstand bench; these benches are made out of wood and generally two to four feet long. The acrobat, usually a woman for this kind of trick, would stand on top of the bench, on top of the vase, on top of my head, and bend backwards to the flowers. That was the general concept. From there, I needed someone to make the equipment. The bench, the vase; everything had to balance perfectly for the trick to work. The vase had to be much, much sturdier than a regular vase—no way could you do this with a household item—and it had to fit properly on my head. One slip and the acrobat on top could tumble to the ground, or land right on my face. That's no good. A father of one of my students worked on the design, and we went through many, many failures.

A lot of people helped us with the equipment. My wife's factory assisted, and the factory where future Nanjing troupe member Xiaohong Weng's father worked pitched in as well. I added choreography to smooth out the process of getting our acrobat from the ground to the bench. Spinning plates, the skill I had spent hours learning outside in the bitter cold, gave our arms something to do. The base (that's the person on the bottom) held three spinning plates on sticks in each hand, while the top held four in each hand as she bent backward to lift the flowers.

It took about six months before "Picking Flowers on Top of a Head" was ready to show. Despite my excitement, I kept my mouth quiet. I was careful not to make a big deal about the new act, or to say too much outside of the group working on it. We performed the trick for the first time—finally!—during a holiday show in Nanjing.

Everything went well. The choreography was smooth, the trick well received. The audience liked it and the professionals liked it. I've always placed a high importance on how other circus and arts professionals perceive a trick; I respect the opinions of people working in the field even more than the audience. Generally, if the professionals think an act is good, the audience will recognize that too.

Both of these tricks I described, kicking the bowls and picking the flowers, continued well past the time when I could do them. The kicking bowls trick is something of a Chinese Acrobatics standard now. You might even see it at half time during a Warriors basketball game. And the picking flowers trick ended up in what I'm told is a very famous American book about juggling, *The Complete Juggler* by Dave Finnigan. I have no idea how it got in there. I don't remember talking to Dave Finnigan or anyone else about an American juggling book. If one of my students had not asked, I wouldn't even know it was there.

Of course, right now, if you know me, you might be thinking, "But Lu Yi, you're leaving out the best one."

Don't worry. I haven't forgotten my most famous trick.

NINE

A 'STUPID' TRICK

The teeterboard head-to-head catch took so long to get right, I gave up on keeping it a secret. Practicing at night for six months was one thing; a year was too much. We started practicing in the daytime. Not that it mattered. I quickly realized that no one wanted to steal that trick. Instead, people tried to talk us out of it. Other performers, even a trainer, discouraged us.

"Give it up," they said. "It's too dangerous."

Maybe I should have listened. In later years, I came to think of the teeterboard head-to-head catch as a "stupid" trick. By that, I mean it's extremely difficult but doesn't necessarily translate to the audience. Only the professionals who see it really understand the difficulty. In that situation, maybe you have to be a little stupid to keep going. Maybe it's smarter to do something easier. But I did not think that way at the time.

I created the head-to-head catch with Xia Ke Min. Even though it strained our relationship, and led to the closest thing we had to a fight, I don't know who else I could have trusted with such an endeavor. The idea, as usual, came from watching other acrobats. Lots of performers on the teeterboard would go high in the air, flying, and come down on another person. They might land in a two-high (that's one person on top of the other, generally with feet landing on shoulders), three-high and so on. Or maybe they would land on a chair, or get caught some other way. But no one had landed a teeterboard head-to-head catch without using their hands. And that's what I wanted to do. It would not be easy.

I was the base, Xia Ke Min the flyer. I would wait for Xia's signal—slapping his legs with straight arms, the teeterboard standard I wrote about earlier—then run to the other end of the teeterboard and jump on it with both feet, making myself heavy and my weight focused on the board. I had to pivot immediately to find Xia in the air. The only thing to lessen the impact of our two skulls colliding was a small donut-like pad held on the top of my head by a chin strap. We practiced and practiced, Xia landing one way then the other. This gave me some headaches, a lot of lost hair, and plenty of stress. It was hard for Xia too. But he understood how much the trick meant, how much recognition it could bring us, and how determined I was, so he followed along. Most of the time.

I talked earlier about Xia's silly side, his tendency to goof around, and how much that helped him for humorous acts, such as the "Happy Chef." But at that time, working on something as difficult as head-to-head on a teeterboard, Xia's good humor frustrated me. He was getting lazy, and that made me mad. Too mad. It's one of those things I regret.

On the day I lost my temper, I was already feeling nervous. I had been hurt on an ugly catch, when I fell over trying to make sure Xia did not land on the ground. It scraped my knees

badly—to the point where you could see my bones. I still have
the scars there. Between the pain and the nerves, I couldn't take
any more of Xia's slacking or playtime antics. After one of our
tries I stormed over to a chair and grabbed it. Not a regular chair,
but a small one, a prop made out of bamboo that we used in our
shows, the kind teeterboard flyers sometimes land in. I raised
the chair and flung it at Xia Ke Min.

I wasn't really aiming at him, or trying to hit him. I was just
angry and frustrated, and it happened almost automatically. Not
that it mattered. Xia was a top-level acrobat with quick reflexes.
He could easily avoid a tossed chair. But I could tell that he felt
bad. We both did. Me for releasing so much anger, and him for
not trying harder. I had promised Xia things would be different
in Nanjing. I told him there would be no more beatings, and now
I was throwing chairs. I'm not proud of that. The whole idea of
the teeterboard head-to-head catch seemed questionable in that
moment. Maybe the trick was impossible. Maybe the other performers and trainers had a point. Maybe we really should give up.
Xia and I took some days away from each other, and then set a
time to meet in my office.

The conversation was short: "Are we going to continue, or
are we going to quit?"

As you can probably guess, we agreed to keep going. And
eventually, the trick worked. We ran through different combinations: two people jump on the teeterboard, three people jump on
the teeterboard. The one that worked best turned out to be just
me, jumping down from a high stool.

Our first time performing the head-to-head catch happened
in Nanjing, as usual for new stuff. It stayed in our repertoire for
years. We landed it at almost every show we tried it in, too. The

only failure happened in Beijing, but it did not dent our reputation to miss it once. The trick brought us much respect within the Chinese Acrobatics community—we were, of course, the first people to do it. As far as I know, we are still the only people to do it. No one has replicated a no-hand teeterboard head-to-head catch since.

Maybe that's because it is too difficult. Or, maybe, it's because most people are too smart to try a "stupid" trick.

TEN

EVERYONE FALLS EVENTUALLY

They arrested me on a Friday, in 1970. I remember it was Friday because it was payday. When I went to get my money, I was told that I could not leave. Luckily, I stayed at the troupe headquarters sometimes, so I had a few simple overnight items there, like a toothbrush and sleeping mat. I gave the money to my mother-in-law to take home and settled down in the office.

It was clear why they detained me. Some people might even say I should have seen it coming, but I did not. The arrest felt like a slap in the face; an unpleasant surprise that caught me off guard. Even after the officials detained me, I still had too much faith. *It's just temporary*, I thought. A short stay in the office. That "short stay" turned into a year of isolation.

The officials who arrested me had come to "oversee" the acrobatic troupe recently. There were seven or eight of them, mostly older, appearing to be in their forties and fifties while we were mostly in our twenties. They knew nothing about acrobatics. They had no background in performance, opera, Chinese arts, or anything. They were people who know nothing. Poor people who did labor work and became radicalized by the Communist Party. They just didn't have any kind of stain in their family history. No ties to the former Nationalist government or to intellectuals. My mistake, if you want to call it that, was arguing with them.

That's how things went during the Cultural Revolution. Any perceived slight to Chairman Mao Zedong could lead to trouble. Any accusation of anti-government bias could get a person fired from their job, imprisoned, or publicly humiliated. "Struggle sessions" were a common Cultural Revolution event. Someone would be forced on a stage with a panel, and a crowd would yell slogans and insults at them. These sessions often devolved into violence. Officials used accusations and threats to go after their political enemies. Working people accused others to deflect attention from themselves. It was a very strange time. One that is hard to understand if you did not live through it.

Right away, these new officials decided that a member of the troupe, Yang Xiao Di, held "anti-revolutionary" views. This made me very angry. I had worked and trained with Yang Xiao Di for most of my life. He joined Pan Yin's circus back in Shanghai around the same time I did; endured the same awful training and beatings. He toured with me across the Eastern Bloc to represent China, and followed the troupe to its new home in Nanjing. Yang Xiao Di was no anti-revolutionary. He had no connections against the government or plans to insult Mao or anything else. He was just a performer; a simple artist; a great acrobatic tumbler who went on to become a great clown.

The officials put a hold on the entire company. No performances, no training, nothing. They took Yang Xiao Di away, and split us into groups to be interrogated, with meetings upon meetings upon meetings. No one complained to me, not openly, or even privately. We did not share our thoughts with each other. Complaining in the open was very dangerous in those days—out of the question, even. But I felt strongly that most troupe members did not appreciate the distraction, or the complete disruption of our artistic life over a bunch of made-up nonsense. And I was stubborn. I was stubborn and I was a leader. I had a responsibility to stand up for my work, my show, my acrobats, and my students. The officials sounded ridiculous and I let them know.

"You have no proof about Yang Xiao Di," I told them. "Nothing."

Of course, my pushback made the meetings take longer. These officials were affiliated with the People's Liberation Army. They did not want any kind of public dissent. They went on and on, talking over everyone, blustering about "illegal" this and "illegal" that. Frustrated, I yelled back: "You guys are illegal!"

That's probably what got me in so much trouble. They stuck me in my office, told me to think about what I had done wrong. But I did not think I had done anything wrong; and I did not think Yang Xiao Di had done anything wrong either. No amount of "thinking" would change that. I stayed in there for about ten days while the officials dragged the rest of the troupe into all those meetings. I don't know exactly what the other acrobats said or did. Probably, they made up a bunch of nonsense the officials wanted to hear, hoping to satisfy them so the whole thing would blow over. Maybe I should have done the same. It would have been easier that way. From my office, I could hear other people leaving, heading home to their families at night, a privilege I was not allowed. My home was only a five-minute walk from the training facility; a nice, unified, three-level building with brick walls and gates in the front and the back. But at night, it felt much farther away.

After that first week and a half, the officials came in the middle of the night and shook me awake. *Time to go.*

They stuffed my few office belongings into a wooden barrel, and drove me to a nearby museum. They gave me a piece of paper with a list of questions to answer, stuff about my mistakes, political ideology, and other nonsense. I filled out the paper and gave it back to them. The officials took the paper, but returned soon after.

"We're not happy," they said. "You need to keep thinking."

Keep thinking. That was always their answer. Keep thinking until you decide to say what we want you to say, whether it's true or not. The limits of my stubborn persona were set to be tested. They had lost interest in reality, and I steadfastly refused political fantasy. "You don't follow Mao," they would say. "You need to keep thinking." The officials assembled a small, makeshift tent, outside on the museum grounds. It had four sleeping spaces, with beds made of hay and a mat thrown on top. One other person, someone I didn't know, stayed in there with me. We did not talk much or get to know each other. There was little to be gained by friendly chatter. The officials wanted us to spend our time "thinking," not talking. That was our main activity. Thinking, and being interrogated.

After a while, I did start thinking, but not really about my alleged political mistakes or my feelings toward Mao. I thought about my newborn daughter Lu Yue. I thought about my wife, left alone with our daughter. I had no way to reach them. No chance to get a message. They might have thought I died. If something bad happened to them, I would have no way to know unless the guards told me. This made me terribly unhappy. I grew very, very sad. I wanted to cry. Sometimes, I grew terribly angry as well. I was thinking, all right. I was thinking how unjust and stupid the whole thing was.

The officials would ask questions to try and lead you into admitting things that never happened, or to find any kind of political dirt in your background. "Tell us what organizations you joined," they would say. "Tell us what activities you did with those organizations."

They wanted me to talk about the May 16 Group, sometimes also called 516. They wanted me to tell them about all of 516's meetings and plans. But it would have been very hard for me to talk about that group. Not just because I was never part of it— but because it did not exist! It was more made-up nonsense. One of the first documents that started the Cultural Revolution was issued by the government on May 16, in 1966. In the years that followed, many stories attached themselves to that date. People would take a small pebble of truth and spin it out into a boulder of conspiracies about clandestine organizations that went against Mao and the government.

The fact that there was no such group posed a challenge to the officials trying to find its members, but it was not insurmountable. They knew how to make people confess. They could beat them; threaten them; torture them; hold them in a tent for a year. Sometimes, they would come to me and say, "We'll let you go if you say you're part of it."

Things dragged on like that for months, with little variation.

Then, out of nowhere, my wife Wang Hong Zhu showed up for a visit. This would have ordinarily been against the rules. But Hong Zhu was clever, and tricked her way past the door.

Here's what happened: While I was being held, my wife was still going to work at a factory. After about six months, someone at the factory wandered up to her and said, "I saw your husband." This person must have had some kind of business at the museum and noticed me in my little tent. Hong Zhu decided to come and have a look. She brought Yue, who was about eight months old, and she brought a good story for the guards.

Naturally, the guards did not want to let her inside.

"I'm here because I lost my key," Hong Zhu told them. "I can't go home."

This was not true (rather like the accusations against me). Hong Zhu knew the exact location of her keys. But she kept pushing. The guards were hesitant. But even for them, it was difficult to turn away a woman holding her infant daughter.

"I know that he has an extra key," Hong Zhu said. "Can I meet my husband to get my key?"

The guards said they would have to check with the supervisor. Hong Zhu waited while they made some calls. Finally, she was allowed inside. They let us meet so I could "give her the key," and they let us talk for a bit. It was a huge relief to see her and Yue, but our conversation felt strained. We had a government minder on each side. Yue had gotten quite skinny. I was worried that this had something to do with my disappearance. That the family was having a difficult time in my absence. As waves of guilt rolled over me, Hong Zhu asked a very pointed question.

"Okay," she said, "admit your wrongdoings. What did you do?"

She wanted me to confess, to give up. That's what was expected of us during the Cultural Revolution. Many people got accused of things they didn't do. Resistance only prolonged their difficulty. But giving up has never been the Lu Yi way. I stayed quiet on the subject of my supposed crimes, only discussing regular, everyday things. But the guards still allowed Hong Zhu to return for visits, about once a week after that first time. Our conversations stayed simple: what was going on at home, stuff like that. Nothing about my so-called errors. Hong Zhu, of course, knew I had not done anything wrong when she tried to get me to confess. She just wanted me to come home. I wanted to go home too. After several months, my resistance started to feel tiring, like a handstand that went on for too long.

When you start to lose control of a handstand, your arms shake. Your neck tenses and sometimes the muscles bulge out. Your hands stop squeezing the floor and instead push the bottom part of the palm into the ground, straining the wrist. Your shoulders sink when they should push up. Your feet tilt, your legs lean over, your hips fold in. Without a break, even the most talented acrobat will collapse from exhaustion if enough time passes. It's only a matter of how long: One minute. Two minutes. Five minutes. Twenty minutes. Sixty-five minutes. Two hours. Everyone falls eventually.

ELEVEN

'REVOLUTIONARY CIRCUS'

It wasn't just the obvious physical threat of being locked up, tortured, or beaten that made the Cultural Revolution such a difficult time. Psychology played a part. The air was thick with constant fear. People turned on each other. As a star acrobat, I was a prime target in those days, but regular people had reason to worry too. For example, my sister Lu Gui Ying worked in a factory. When her son was accused of anti-government activities, she could not face the terror of accusatory officials and angry mobs. She killed herself by drinking pesticide.

This news saddened me deeply. And it made me angry. I spent much of the time in that makeshift jail angry. I would get so mad that my hands would shake—they were so unsteady I could barely write on the papers the guards handed me. That problem stuck around for decades. Even in America, sometimes I would hold a pencil to paper and flash back to the Cultural Revolution, with those angry jitters shaking my hands.

I have always liked to keep trying, keep working, keep pushing. I have always wanted to do better, to do more. But no one can do every trick. If you're very short and very skinny, it will be hard to be a base—maybe it's better to do hand-balancing. If you're thick and tall, it might be hard to tumble—probably better to be a base. And if you've been in isolation for a year, it's better to go home. The officials kept asking about the May 16 Group. It became quite obvious I could bring this sad chapter to an end if I "admitted" my activities. So, finally, that's what I did.

"Yes," I told the interrogators. "I participated in 516."

I told them about our meetings; where we held them; what we talked about. All made up. Nothing that actually happened. After my "confession," the officials told me that Yang Xiao Di and Xia Ke Min had also confessed, and admitted to joining 516. I guess I had been associating with counter-revolutionaries all along. Who knew the circus could be such an intellectually dangerous place? Maybe our minds got confused from standing upside-down all day.

The whole idea of anti-government acrobats was ridiculous. Even if we wanted to, our schedules didn't allow time for subversive plots. We had too much training, too many rehearsals, and too many shows. But the story got me out of isolation. I could say goodbye to the guards, the museum, the tent, the constant "thinking." I could go home.

The officials, of course, could not let me leave without an acknowledgement of my errors. I was, after all, a confessed conspirator in the dreaded "Counterrevolutionary May 16 Conspiracy." They held a raid at my house, followed by a big meeting to criticize me. This was more of the same conversations, about political thought and following Mao and all the anti-government stuff I did against the party. But at least it happened at home. And when it was over, I was done. I was back with my own family, my own walls, my own bed. That's always better than a tent with a cook and a guard.

After my release, the circus slowly returned to its activities. We started with something pretty silly: "Revolutionary Circus." These were patriotic shows designed for the sensibilities of the Cultural Revolution. It started in Beijing and spread through the country. All the troupes participated: dance, opera, and various cultural organizations. Performers dressed as soldiers and pretended to fight our supposed foreign enemies of the time, mainly the Japanese and Americans. Our troupe mostly fought Americans.

We kept the tricks pretty simple for these shows. They had to be simple, because people had lost their skills during the long break. We couldn't do any serious acrobatics. Only funny stuff and general performing: easy magic tricks; light tumbling; and basic partner work, like a two-high where the top climbs onto the base's shoulders with a pretend gun. He aims it around, ready to shoot the imperialist enemies. Dive rolls to the ground to escape incoming gunfire. That kind of stuff.

The revolutionary circus shows were a bit of a chore, but they were kind of fun too. We laughed at the silliness of it all, and used the exercise as a warm-up for real shows. It felt good to be doing something again. To be performing and moving around, instead of sitting and thinking all day. It was like the sun finally coming up after a long, strange season of darkness.

As frightening, distressing, and mind-numbing as my time as a prisoner was, it could have been worse. Much worse. I had it better than most people who were arrested during the Cultural Revolution. My interrogators never beat, tortured, or killed me. I didn't find out until later, but the people holding me had been told I was useful, and the local officials in Nanjing did not want the leader of their city's prized circus sent away to some distant farm or labor camp. So they could not treat me too poorly. I always had food. I never starved. Maybe that doesn't sound like "special" treatment now, but it helped me survive at the time. It was probably a big part of why the guards allowed my wife to visit.

Most of my guards also knew I had done nothing wrong, so they were not too harsh. The officials didn't have any kind of strict system for who could watch me. They just picked people at random. I even knew some of them. One, Chu Fu Shen, was a student of mine at the acrobatic troupe. Another was the cook who made all of our meals; and another came from the department of culture.

Not long ago, someone asked me what I think about the Cultural Revolution now. They asked if I would say anything to those officials who arrested me. The truth is, I wouldn't say much. There's nothing I have to say to any particular individual. The Cultural Revolution was a movement that encompassed the whole country. Things came down from the top. People did what they needed to survive.

Lots of smart people—scholars, professors, journalists—have written about why the Cultural Revolution happened. You can read those books if you want to know more. My opinion is that the Cultural Revolution happened because Mao wanted to secure his power. He wanted to use his movement to get rid of potential rivals. He almost got rid of my acrobatic troupe too. But, looking back, I can see that I was lucky. I survived.

TWELVE

DRIVING OUTBACK

There is one thing I did in Australia that I have never done since—I drove a car. I had never learned to drive. I never needed to, because everything is taken care of in the circus. We took trains and planes or had drivers. Learning to drive never seemed like a priority. But I tried it that one time in Australia, just for fun.

This would have been around 1984. We had already been to Australia a year or so before for a performance tour booked by an Australian agency. Our shows helped us build a reputation, so we were invited back, this time by the local Asian community, to train Australian people in Chinese Acrobatics. This was a big deal at the time. Chinese performers mostly stayed in China or performed in other socialist-friendly countries. The Australians even made a documentary about our trip, and it won a film award.

Our troupe went to all the major cities: Melbourne, Adelaide, Sydney, and even Perth, which is very far away from the rest of the country. The idea to drive a car came around because one of our students had a big open patch of land. Australia has a lot of open space. Compared to the United States, the middle of the country is practically empty. It was perfect for a beginner driver. I also rode a horse on that property. I still have a photo of that somewhere.

Xia Ke Min already knew how to drive, so he took us out there. He parked, then we switched places. I thought about the pedals and the steering wheel. *Gas on the right, brake on the left. Turn the wheel where you want to go.* I didn't have to think about which side of the road to drive on, because we were out in the middle of nowhere, with no roads. I pushed the gas and watched the land roll by past the window. I liked it right away. *Feels relaxing after work*, I thought.

After that, I did think about getting a car and learning to drive for real. But I never got around to it. Life with the acrobatic troupe kept me pretty busy. Much later, after I got settled in the U.S., I thought about it again. People rely much more on cars in America, so it would have made sense. But by that time I was sixty years old, and my daughters said I was too old. I had already missed the opportunity.

I didn't realize this at the time, but the workshops we taught in Australia offered me a preview of what working with students in America would be like. In China, people train for money, for a chance at a better life, and the training is very bitter. But Western students train for love. That's what it was like in Australia. The people did not have a lot of acrobatic skills. Most of them could juggle balls or do some simple tumbling. But they wanted to get better, so they pushed themselves. They were very eager to be on the stage.

The students in our workshop came from all over Australia, selected by the government. They did not have to pay for training. We stayed for three months teaching handstands, stretching,

59

tumbling, teeterboard, and meteors (that's a trick where acrobats spin a long rope with bowls of water attached at the ends. You can attach round balls to the rope instead, which is better for beginners). At the end of the term, we had a big performance for everyone to show their skills. By then, our coaches had gotten close to the students, and the students had gotten close to us. Emotions ran pretty high at the final performance. The Australian prime minister came—and, I'm proud to say, the students had improved dramatically during our lessons. Many people cried at the show; audience members, performers, even one of our trainers. I felt emotional but managed not to cry. I don't cry in public very often. In this book, it only happens once.

Before we went home to China, one of the students gave me a drawing. It was of me, focused on training, with a bit of a frown, and pointing at something. This particular student tended to act a bit naughty. He was very smart but did not focus well, so I often tried to push him. In the small drawing, I could only assume I was pointing at him, telling him to focus.

Several years later I went to see Circus Oz in Berkeley. Circus Oz is a show from Australia known for rock music and wild humor. As the show went on, I recognized one of the clowns. He did a little bit of everything, covering transitions the way clowns so often do: a trick on the pole; a flash of skill on the bicycle; a handstand on the chair. After a while, I realized where I had seen this clown before. He was that same naughty boy who created a drawing of me back in Australia. I guess he turned his inability to focus on any one thing into a pretty good job, doing lots of different things.

THIRTEEN

THE BIG APPLE CIRCUS
MEETS NANJING

It's not enough to be good.

Talent is a beginning, a basic. But you need more. Sometimes you need luck, and yes, I know you can't create luck. One thing you can create? Relationships. In order to be successful, you also have to build relationships. A well-placed friend or connection can make all the difference. I'll give you an example.

Late in the 1980s, a friend and associate in Beijing, Xu Su'E, contacted me about an American circus producer on a mission. Paul Binder, co-founder and ringmaster of the Big Apple Circus in New York City, wanted his show to be the first American circus to book Chinese acrobats in the U.S. And he was coming to China to find those acrobats.

You may be familiar with the Big Apple Circus from their holiday shows at Lincoln Center in Manhattan, or from Barry Lubin's famous "Grandma" clown character. I had not seen either of those things at the time. But I knew their reputation, I knew I wanted to book the Nanjing Acrobatic Troupe in America, and I knew Xu Su'E would help. We had worked together before and carried similar feelings about circus and performance. So in this case I had the talent, with my troupe; I had the relationship, with Xu Su'E; and I even had a bit of luck—it turned out that Xu Su'E would be one of the guides taking Paul Binder around to look at acrobatic troupes.

Xu Su'E watched Paul Binder closely. He took note of his comments and body language to figure out what Paul Binder liked and didn't like. He figured out what Paul Binder was looking for. And he reported back when, after the initial round of auditions, Paul Binder was still not satisfied with the options.

"Get him to Nanjing," I told Xu Su'E, "and I'll show him what we have."

I rearranged my acts. Paul Binder apparently liked the very traditional Chinese numbers. The lion dance, the dragon dance, things that have been around for thousands of years. A lot of troupes had quit doing those acts. I made sure to highlight them.

Paul Binder arrived in Nanjing with Dominique Jando, a French clown who has since become a circus historian. I would work with him again several years later, at the circus school in San Francisco. An official from the Chinese culture department brought the two of them to our acrobatic headquarters, and we started the show. Paul Binder picked our troupe on the spot. Right away, we started discussing how to integrate the two companies. Conveniently, I had set up a dinner at my house.

We took Paul Binder over to my house in the troupe's car, which I was very proud of at the time. No other acrobatic troupe in the country had a personal car. Authorization to purchase it came down from the top, as a reward for representing China overseas. The money came from the shows we made on those trips. We bought it new, a minivan with four seats, and a beige-cream, pearl-white paint on the outside body. It was domestic and quite nice, no rattling or broken seat belts or anything like that. Of course, I never actually drove this vehicle. Its condition was too good to risk putting someone like me behind the wheel. The troupe hired a full-time driver for our little van. He drove Paul Binder and Dominique Jando to the dinner.

This dinner was truly impressive. Wang Hong Zhu did most of the cooking, and did it very, very well. There was so much food we couldn't fit all the dishes on the table! Fish, shrimp, salted duck, pork belly with preserved vegetables, and the Nanjing version of sweet and sour pork, with the dark brown sauce used in our region, made from Chinese vinegar and sugar (not that red sauce you always see in America). Xu Su'E told me Paul Binder liked spicy foods and pork belly, so I made sure we had plenty of both. We went all-out, Chinese style, to impress the American circus producer, and it worked. In the following days, Paul Binder and I had many great discussions about our upcoming collaboration.

The entire Big Apple Circus could not come to China for a visit, so live rehearsal was impossible. But we talked about how the stage might look, how to mix American circus with Chinese Acrobatics, what kind of characters might be in the show, all those things. Paul Binder was interested in the character of the Monkey King, which fit our theme of East-meets-West. The Monkey King comes from the classic Chinese novel *Journey to the West*. It's a fictionalized version of a pilgrimage taken during the Tang dynasty by a monk named Xuanzang, who went through many travails on his journey from China to India in search of ancient Buddhist texts. In the novel, the monk is accompanied by magical characters who serve as protectors and disciples. The Monkey King is the most memorable and famous of these characters, featured over the centuries in Chinese opera, plays, films, television, and even video games. The Monkey King uses all sorts of physical and mental magic; he zips, zaps, dives, and flies. A perfect character for an acrobatic circus.

I gathered a lot of information about the American market from talking with Paul Binder. Americans, it seemed, like things bigger. The more spectacular, the better. I reworked the lion dance so our performers tumbled around the entire stage instead of just part of it, and I made the structure the lion jumps onto much taller. I think Paul Binder learned a bit from working with us too. American circuses, as I would soon find out, had lots of good clowns and animal acts, but not so much in the way of high-level acrobatics. I think seeing Chinese Acrobatics up close gave him a sense of the vast potential of the human body, and of Chinese training methods. You could say our time together was mutually beneficial, as all great collaborations should be. We signed an agreement for three years. The plan was to have holiday performances in New York in the winter and tours around the eastern United States during the warmer months.

The Big Apple Circus Meets the Monkey King opened its first run in New York City in December 1988. We picked Yang Xiao Di to play the Monkey King, and he excelled in the role. Yang Xiao Di always liked to act. Traditional Chinese Acrobatics is all skills and tricks, so this gave him a chance to mix in character work and have a little more fun. He could tumble across the stage and be silly, interacting with the American clowns. In one memorable number, Yang Xiao Di traded tricks with John Lepiarz, who contrasted the white face and flowing, bright yellow garments of the Monkey King character by dressing as a baseball fan, with shaggy hair, baggy pants, a loose blue-and-white Brooklyn jersey and a baseball glove on one hand.

The usual performance went like this: Yang Xiao Di opens the act with a few plate tricks, and John Lepiarz stylishly tosses a baseball around. They go back and forth a few times, before the American clown uses one of Yang Xiao Di's plates to catch his baseball from a high toss. With an air of mischief, Yang Xiao Di hands the American clown an egg, as if to say: "Oh yeah? Well, try it with this!" John Lepiarz does the same high toss and catches the egg on the plate. Yang Xiao Di takes the egg back, puts a thin stick on his nose, and balances the egg on the end of the stick. Then he adds another egg. And then one more, until he has three eggs balanced on the stick on his nose. The act ends with Yang Xiao Di wildly tossing an egg toward John Lepiarz, who has no chance of catching it on the plate but tries anyway. The egg shatters, the audience laughs, and the two clowns take their leave.

In both American and Chinese circus, it's common to have the funny acts perform during transitions. In America, you might picture a clown with a pie in their face, or a pile of clowns coming out of a car. But look closely behind those clowns, and someone is probably setting up a teeterboard, or a trapeze, or a pair of Chinese poles. We did the same thing in the Big Apple Circus show. The American clowns and Yang Xiao Di kept the audience interested—during those moments where you need to set something up, or take something down—with laughs, silliness and light acrobatics. Whenever possible, the transition number should have some connection to the act.

To use the example from a moment ago, when John Lepiarz and Yang Xiao Di finished their egg and plate routine, they moved to the side of the stage, and extended their arms toward the curtain. It opened to reveal seven of our women acrobats, who were all spinning plates on long sticks, four in each hand. So the clowns' plate and egg act transitioned seamlessly into the plate spinning act. In that number, the acrobats walk, roll around, hold elbow stands, hold head stands, and hold head stands on top of other acrobats—all while spinning eight plates. The finale is the "Picking Flowers on Top of a Head" trick I secretly worked on back in Nanjing. But I wasn't the base anymore. By this time, I had moved on from performing to directing. Chinese acrobats retire quite early.

The Big Apple Circus Meets the Monkey King wasn't a total theatrical experience like the shows that Cirque du Soleil would make so famous in North America a few years later, but it was groundbreaking in its own way to bring these Chinese performers to an American-style circus—and right in the heart of New York City. Paul Binder has always credited his Big Apple Circus as the first show to bring Chinese Acrobatics to the American circus. And as far as I know, he's correct. That first run was very good for both troupes. The Big Apple Circus raised its reputation by introducing Chinese Acrobatics to Americans. And the Nanjing Acrobatic Troupe found more interest for booking performances and tours overseas after that contract. Yang Xiao Di made some good friends among the American clowns, which surely helped him in later years when he joined another New York show; he went on to a long, successful performance career in America. I believe he is still in New York today.

All of this might never have happened without the keen eyes and willing help of a good colleague in Beijing. Let that serve as an example of why you should always be polite, fair, and honest in your business or artistic dealings. You never know who could help you later!

Of course, if you know me, or even a little bit about the Lu Yi story, you know that the second Big Apple Circus trip, when we went back for the summer tour, created some serious problems for my position: with the troupe, with the Chinese government, with everything. You could say that tour was like a circus act with an equipment malfunction right before the finale. Everything went great—until the very end.

FOURTEEN

A JOURNEY TO THE WEST

When we first arrived, everyone was excited to land in New York City. It was a new experience: Times Square, the Statue of Liberty—all those famous landmarks. New York seemed very modern, very happening. The troupe took a short break, and then we had a week to put the show together. This left little time for exploration. That was okay, because our attempts at exploration did not go so well. It turned out that we did not live in the most modern, happening part of New York. We stayed in trailers, far out in Brooklyn.

We were surprised to discover that American cities could be quite dangerous, and you had to be careful at night. For people who wanted to explore the neighborhood, our policy was to go out in groups of three. One of our groups found trouble early on. Someone on the street purposely ran into an acrobat, then fell over, faking that they broke a bone. It was some kind of street scam to get money. There were also prostitutes who would grab people. They would latch on to a man in the group and try to drag him into a building, very aggressively. Coming from China, we were not used to this type of stuff.

None of this really mattered, though, because we spent most of our time on the show. That's circus life. Even once the performances started, we would stay an hour after to work extra. That hour was time for anyone to work on new skills or tricks. And you always need new tricks.

The real challenge for me started later, on a very famous date: June 4, 1989. Lots of people in China refer to it as the "June 4 Incident." Americans usually say "Tiananmen Square Incident," or maybe the "Tiananmen Square Massacre." In some ways, it was similar to what happened in Budapest. Thousands of people, many of them students who wanted less corruption and more personal freedom, gathered in Tiananmen Square in Beijing for weeks. This made the government feel threatened. China is not like the United States, where you can say whatever you want about the government. It's not like that at all.

On June 4, the government sent the military—still the People's Liberation Army—to end the protests and clear Tiananmen Square. The army fired into the crowd. They killed civilians, unarmed people, peaceful protestors. Some army soldiers were killed too, by demonstrators who fought back with homemade weapons. But most of the deaths were among the protestors. Some demonstrators even got run over by tanks. It was a horrible, grisly scene. One that, thankfully, I only had to see on TV. New York Channel 7.

We kept a big TV in the room where we rested between shows. It was always on, always showing something, so of course everyone saw what happened. It was hard to watch those reports, to see people running, vehicles burning in the streets. It made me very sad, for those people and for our country. But at the same time, I wasn't convinced it was real. *It's America, things are different here,* I thought. *You see all kinds of news here, and it's all negative.* I thought it might be fake. Maybe. At the same time, my mind processed that something might happen with the troupe. *Now some people won't want to go back.* That was my first thought.

This idea weighed on me for the rest of the tour. As the leader, I was considered responsible for the group. I left with a troupe of seventeen people. The government and the culture department would expect me to come back with the same number. It was my job, my responsibility. My reputation. No one in the troupe said anything to me about a plan to defect. But there had been other incidents, other troupes that went overseas and had performers disappear. And we were in America, after all. The possibility to defect was always out there, floating in the air.

When I had a chance, I gathered the troupe together for a general discussion.

"Let's go back home," I told them. "And if you want to come out again, I will help you."

I offered to get the process rolling. I had done this before, I said. One of my performers in Australia wanted to stay there. I helped this person come back to China, go through all the right procedures, and then go back to Australia. It worked better that way. The legal way. I wanted the troupe to trust me. To believe I would help them as much as possible. But defecting, I said, "This is not legal."

Still, no one mentioned a plan to leave. They kept it a tight secret. But I suspected. I could smell it cooking, like oil in a pan. Soon after that meeting I looked in the mirror. All of a sudden, gray hairs seemed to be sprouting everywhere.

We made it through the whole tour before anything happened. On the last night, in Vermont, after the final show, I noticed some passports were missing. Six passports, five that belonged to performers and one that belonged to our translator, He Lanrong. If people planned to defect, it made perfect sense that He Lanrong would be involved. No one in the troupe spoke good English except for her. But, oddly enough, He Lanrong was still there the following morning, as if she had been left behind. I sent two people to keep watch on her, Yang Xiao Di and Qui Bing Chuan, one of our acrobats who mostly did group numbers. They found He Lanrong attempting to sneak away and confronted her.

I don't know exactly what happened there, but it ended like this: Yang Xiao Di and Qui Bing Chuan got He Lanrong into the circus bus, the one for the Nanjing Acrobatic Troupe. She was not happy, and neither were we, but the trip back to New York commenced. It's about a five- or six-hour drive from Vermont to Brooklyn, more if you're a whole circus caravan. Someone, somewhere—maybe one of the Americans—called the police on the way, and they followed us to Brooklyn.

Yang Xiao Di and I were furious with the translator and the defectors. It felt like they had betrayed us. The contract with Big Apple Circus was supposed to last three years, and we had just finished the first tour. There was so much more to come. These defectors stood poised to ruin everything. All of our hard work and effort thrown out the window, left to rot in the sun like garbage. And for what? We had already come to the U.S., gone back to China, and come back to the United States once. There was no reason to think we wouldn't be able to do so again. The June 4 Incident was truly terrible, but it seemed like an excuse. Like they were looking for a reason to defect and found one. As a prominent, high-level acrobatic troupe, we enjoyed a good position in China and had no reason to suspect our lives would be different than before.

I had asked the troupe to trust me, and these six people refused. But there was nothing I could do. We got back to Brooklyn and the police told He Lanrong she could stay in America if she wanted. So that's what she did. As for the others, I hadn't seen them all day. Their plan to evade and fool me worked. Simple as that.

Later, I went to the Chinese consulate to seek assistance and advice. They only pretended to help. No one at the consulate wanted to get involved. They didn't want to take on any of the responsibility. If the Nanjing Acrobatic Troupe lost some people, it was better for everyone if Lu Yi took the blame. There was no escape from that. I could only lower my shoulders and go home; same as I would after a long day of training with no success.

Soon after, we boarded the long flight back to China. As Manhattan, Times Square, and the Statue of Liberty got smaller and smaller, I could only say goodbye. Goodbye, Statue of Liberty; goodbye, Big Apple Circus contract; and goodbye to some unknown portion of Lu Yi's reputation for excellence. China awaits your return.

FIFTEEN

BACK TO CHINA, BACK TO NEW YORK

The Nanjing Acrobatic Troupe had come to expect a bit of fanfare upon our return from an overseas trip. A "Welcome Home" banner and a crowd to greet us at the airport. The vice mayor of Nanjing would attend and congratulate us personally. But this time, after our second trip to the United States? Very different. No vice mayor, no fanfare. Nothing. The silence said it all. Our troupe would carry guilt by association. We consorted with defectors, and would take the blame.

This struck me as unfair. Our troupe should still be welcomed back. After all, the people who returned were the ones who decided not to defect. Why blame us? We had no control over the authorities in America. No method to stop those people. Naturally, most eyes and the greatest responsibility shifted in my direction. I was the leader.

As soon as we got back, officials from the department of culture came to the troupe's headquarters and oversaw three days of meetings. Meetings in the offices. Meetings in the training space. Meetings everywhere. They resembled "self-criticism" sessions, where people had to say what they did wrong and how they would improve. Meetings like this feel pretty stupid when you haven't done anything wrong, but these were considered absolutely mandatory for anyone who went to the U.S. You could not ask for time off. You could not ask for absence. "Everyone has to attend" was the official word. But I can't tell you what happened there. I actually managed to get out of it—because I had other meetings!

Also around this time, I was supposed to go to Russia. The trip had been scheduled a long time before all the controversy and would have been inconvenient to cancel. So off I went to Russia, which turned out to be quite a disappointment. The country had regressed since my last visit, in 1965. The troupes had lost talent. Their training techniques had regressed. Even the hotels were terrible, with cockroaches coming out of the corners all the time. In circus, you could say there is a certain amount of rivalry between Chinese and Russian acrobatics. We both have long-standing traditions and methods. They are similar, but different in important ways, with each having unique specialties. Of course, I think Chinese Acrobatics is better, and I want us to rise above everyone on the international stage. But it does not make me happy to see a great acrobatic tradition wither. That's no good for anyone.

I came home to more bad news, two pieces of it. First, my handling of the New York trip had been roundly criticized at a national meeting in Beijing. This was an annual meeting for high-level officials from departments of culture across the country. A conference—do your reports, exchange ideas, stuff like that. People at the meeting critiqued me because of the defections; and because I tried to prevent them; and because the police got involved. Basically, if Lu Yi did it, it was wrong. Apparently, I was supposed to take people overseas but keep them from defecting without actually trying to keep them from defecting all while preventing the authorities in a foreign country from interfering. They were mad that I tried to stop the translator, and mad that the translator defected. Somehow, both things were my fault now. Quite a few friends and colleagues attended this meeting and thought the comments were unfair. That's how I heard about it.

The second piece of news was even worse.

In my absence, the department of culture decided I would not be allowed to travel overseas anymore. This was an official government order, a national document given to the local authorities. You can probably guess why. They said I did not lead the team properly in the U.S., because people defected. A travel ban created an obvious problem for someone who leads an acrobatic troupe that is actively seeking contracts overseas, a troupe known for representing China to the world. It was like being fired without actually being fired. Very frustrating. But, as with acrobatic training, sometimes the only option is to keep trying. I kept my ears tuned for a chance at redemption and, sure enough, an opportunity soon arrived.

China is a huge country. For all the power of the government, it can sometimes be complicated to manage. And in this case, that worked to my advantage. The local officials decided to, we'll say, "ignore" the no-travel mandate. They did not want to lose a prestigious, three-year contract with an American circus over a handful of defectors. They let me go back to New York alone. The plan was to find the defectors and convince them to come back and apply to leave China legally, with my help. From there, I would salvage the relationship between the Big Apple Circus and the Nanjing Acrobatic Troupe, and with it the contract. Nothing in this plan worked.

I flew to New York—hello again, Statue of Liberty—but could only find the translator. And we only talked briefly.

I met He Lanrong in the Big Apple Circus office. Things had not gone well for her either. When she defected, she expected to become the agent of the acrobats who left the troupe. But that did not work out. Now, all she wanted to talk about was the situation in China. She wanted to know how she was perceived there. I got the feeling she wanted to come back, but was worried. This might have worked to my advantage if I could find the others. But He Lanrong snapped shut when I asked.

"No," she said. "I haven't talked to them."

This, I could not believe. It seemed unrealistic that a group of acrobats who didn't speak English and needed her help to defect had stopped talking to her. More likely, she just didn't want to say. He Lanrong continued to ask how she might be viewed in China. But I didn't want to say much. I didn't want her going back to China and quoting me; nor did I want any supposedly "improper" things I said to come back to me later.

"I don't know about that," I told her. "Because I'm not in Beijing."

A conversation where one person is quiet and the other says very little is destined to be short. I left the office, no better off than before.

In the weeks that followed, I hung around New York to look for the other defectors. But I'm an acrobat, not a detective. I found a couple of minor clues. Like, "Oh, I saw that person at the supermarket." Nothing concrete, though. No addresses or phone numbers. In the end, I could not track them down. I also had no luck fixing the contract with the Big Apple Circus. I talked about technical stuff with them and helped out with a few acts, but it was too late to save our business relationship.

This was a confusing, difficult period. I was alone in New York City, and stuck between two very different cultures—both of which seemed to blame me for problems I did not create and could not solve. Acrobatics, in some ways, is simple. You train hard for a long time. Slowly, you get better. With more training, you keep getting better until, eventually, your body says "enough," and you find another job; something like teaching, or directing, or office work, because those things use the mind more than the body. An acrobat's life is something I can understand. Something I can help guide and shape. But people and governments and contracts are complicated. I cannot fix those things. Maybe someone else could.

Soon, though, I would run across a reason for optimism. One of those moments where the path splits, forcing you to pick a direction, and then your life changes completely.

SIXTEEN

'HELLO,' AND GOODBYE

T here is a certain magical energy backstage after a good show. Everyone feels lighter. More awake. Alive to the possibilities of the future; thankful to see their hard, often bitter, training rewarded. It doesn't always happen. Some nights feel more like the end of a regular workday. But, on the good nights, the room fills with the hum of laughter, relief, and celebration. There are always extra people hanging around backstage after a show, and more of them turn up on a good night. You might have an old acquaintance say hello. Or meet the friends and family of a performer. Possibly a local celebrity, an important official, or a politician. It seems they can feel that special magic in the air, too. It was on one of those nights, after a Big Apple Circus show in Long Island, New York, that I first met Judy Finelli.

Judy Finelli worked with a group called the Pickle Family Circus in San Francisco, and had flown out to see our show. I didn't know much about the Pickle Family Circus or Judy Finelli, who, I later learned, was a talented juggler and clown. But I was always happy to meet another circus producer—and always keeping an ear out for future bookings. Judy Finelli told me she hoped there would be an opportunity for the Pickles to work with our acrobats. At that point, our contract with the Big Apple Circus was still expected to last three years, so nothing was possible. But I was optimistic. Maybe we could finish our contract with the Big Apple Circus, and then move on to the Pickle Family Circus.

Of course, that did not work out. Instead, I ended up in New York City playing detective. One day, in the middle of that fruitless search, a friend named Cui Bei Su contacted me. He happened to be living in the Bay Area and was in touch with Judy Finelli. Cui Bei Su arranged a meeting for us. By this time, I was set to go back to China but I had a layover in San Francisco. Judy agreed to come talk to me at the airport. You could still go through security without a plane ticket back then, so it was very convenient. But the meeting turned out to be very, very brief. We only managed to exchange one word.

On the day of my journey, I was dismayed to learn that I had some company. The Chinese government sent two handlers to "accompany" me on the trip. People to watch me—like guards— and make sure I got back on the plane. This was upsetting. I came to the U.S. to try and fix things, and now the officials wanted to treat me like a troublemaker. Like a disloyal person who couldn't be trusted on his own. I had always been so proud to represent China. But the bureaucracy, the politics, the weight of blame for things I couldn't help; it was all pushing down on me, like a heavy doubles partner. My mind and spirit felt weary. The official minders followed me through the San Francisco airport.

Judy arrived as planned. But I could not speak to her. It would make everything worse. The men guarding me stood ready to intervene. They would get between us. They would cover my mouth and drag me onto the plane if needed. In that case, someone might call the American police, but that would only extend my troubles, as it did before. I would come in for more criticism back home, and more "self-criticism" for sure. I would probably be prevented from leaving the country again, this time for real. Judy must have seen something on my face, because she played it cool.

She acknowledged me with a wave. I waved back. She got close enough to say one thing: "Hello." I said it back. The officials looked at us, but stayed quiet.

That was the end of our meeting. I got on the plane and went home to China.

Despite the lack of any real discussion, this brief encounter planted a seed of possibility in my mind. A seed that would eventually flourish into a large tree, with many branches of opportunity.

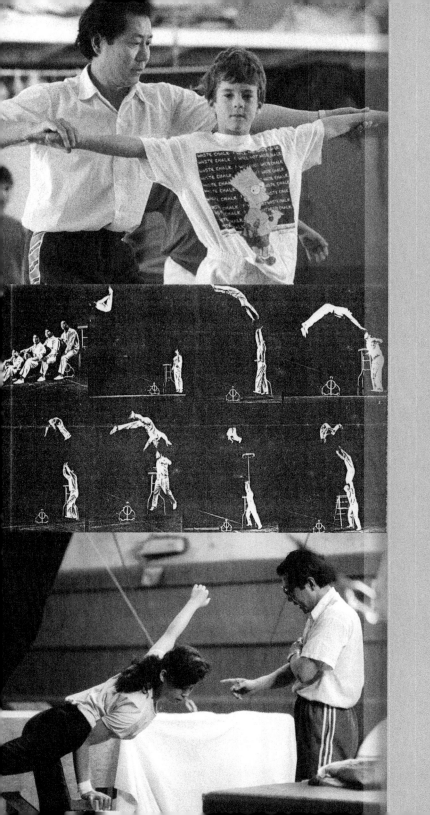

INTERMISSION

FROM 'HUNDRED ENTERTAINMENTS' TO *SALTIMBANCO*: A NOT-SO-BRIEF HISTORY OF CHINESE ACROBATICS

BY DEVIN HOLT

Art rarely stays in one place. One can see this literally—say "traveling circus" to just about anybody and they get a near-instant mental image—and figuratively, in that circus, acrobatics, clowning, dance, music, literature, painting, and anything else you might think of has evolved, changed, twisted, flipped, stretched and been remixed over and over since its invention. Popularity, accolades, and, crucially, funding come and go for any art form. But change, that constant need to improve, to carry forward, to create, never leaves. The artist must travel, both to the audience and toward a higher standard, with every performance, concert, demonstration, or display. And they must face that task whether the times, the culture, the people—the banks!—recognize their work or not.

Some time periods are clearly better for artists than others: Hip-hop fans often reminisce about its "Golden Age" in the late 1980s to mid-'90s. Film buffs might harken back to the days of silent movies, or the output of the studio system that created classic Hollywood films from the 1920s to '60s. Those moments, when talent meets investment, are somewhat rare. Few artists get to live through them. Lu Yi is one who did.

That's not to say that Lu Yi had it easy or got lucky. He most certainly did not. But he does exemplify the old adage about good things happening when talent, hard work, and preparation meet opportunity. Lu Yi was born on September 25, 1939, in harsh, difficult circumstances. But those difficult circumstances also came with a small blessing: His formative acrobatic years coincided with a time when the Chinese government planned to "let a hundred flowers bloom," at least where acrobatics was concerned.

There is plenty to critique about the years following the Communist takeover of China and the founding of the People's Republic in 1949, which supporters called "liberation," or the creation of "New China." Campaigns against intellectuals; a push for "thought reform"; a famine that led to an estimated thirty to fifty million deaths; the Cultural Revolution and its widespread abuses, denunciations, and political killings.

It is necessary to acknowledge the human toll of those tragedies—extensive analysis and explanations of which this writer leaves to more talented experts, ones the interested reader can easily find. But that acknowledgement comes with a recognition that, despite such human rights abuses, the post-liberation Chinese government supported and encouraged a flourishing, vibrant class of professional acrobatic performers. With the notable exception of the Cultural Revolution, the Chinese acrobatic arts, and living conditions for many of its performers, improved in the early years of the

People's Republic of China. The late Premier Zhou Enlai took a personal interest in the art form.

According to *Chinese Acrobatics Through the Ages*, a 1985 book by Fu Qifeng published by the Foreign Languages Press, Premier Zhou assembled a roster of talented acrobats in Beijing in 1950. They were drawn from Shanghai, Tianjin, Beijing, Wuhan, and Shenyang. The acrobats performed in Huairen Hall in Zhongnanhai, Beijing, the new political center of the country. Fu Qifeng describes, "The items presented were wholesome, possessing simplicity and grace, and richly tinged with national characteristics." A clue as to why the new government threw its support behind acrobatics can be found in those last two words, "national characteristics." Acrobatic shows would demonstrate an impressive, traditional Chinese art without any risk of anti-party messaging. Acrobatics is not an art form that lends itself to overt political messaging with the same ease as literature, theater, or opera. At least, not the type of political messaging that critiques an authoritarian regime.

Chairman Mao Zedong and other high-ranking officials decided to start a national troupe, one that could tour to Europe. These acrobats would carry a political message of success for the new government with their presence, but not with the content of their shows. Zhou Enlai named it Zhonghua (China) Acrobatic Troupe, and it later became the China Acrobatic Troupe of Beijing. This was followed by a quick succession of new troupes set up across the country, adding up to some two hundred troupes within a few years (there was even an amateur acrobatic troupe comprised of postal workers that specialized in group bicycle numbers). Mao and Zhou were far from the first of China's leaders to recognize the diplomatic potential of the country's talented acrobats. China's acrobatic tradition stretches back farther than the modern circus, well before the three-ring extravaganzas of the Ringling Brothers, the famed cabarets of Europe, or even the 1760s equestrian antics of Philip Astley—performed in London as the horses galloped through his circular ring, leading to use of the term "circus," for circle, and making him the West's "father of modern circus." What we so often call "Chinese circus" here in the U.S. predates use of the word itself.

Acrobatics appeared in China as early as the Xia Dynasty, in the 17th century, B.C. That's around the same time the last wooly mammoths became extinct. By the time of the Qin (221-206 B.C.) and Han (206 B.C.-220 A.D.) dynasties, acrobatics had "developed into (a) comprehensive art form popular among both royalty and commoners," according to another book by Fu Qifeng, written with Li Xining, *A Primer of Chinese Acrobatics*.

The first leader to present acrobatics at a state function in China was Emperor Wu of the Han Dynasty from 141 B.C. to 87 B.C. The banquet happened in 108 B.C. Emperor Wu aimed to wow emissaries from the "western regions"—these include Xinjiang and Central Asia on today's map—with what was then called the "Hundred Entertainments" or "Feats of the Strange and Wonderful," names that suit modern conceptions of the circus better than the word "circus" itself. These strange, wonderful feats would have included general acrobatics, juggling, plate spinning—quite new at the time—music, theater, opera, magic, and traditional folk art demonstrations like "Horn Butting Games," a type of helmeted wrestling contest influenced by ancient legends.

The roots of the skills developed for the Hundred Entertainments lay mostly in sports, religion, or that oldest of feelings, boredom. There were contests of strength, as with the Horn Butting Games; rituals that grew into performances, including "Jar Tricks" and handstands; and amusements developed from playing with everyday items, like juggling. In China, the "Juggling Boards" grew from the use of boomerangs for hunting. It took a lot of skill to hunt with a boomerang. Over time, hunters developed a range of tricks, which they would demonstrate at fairs, harvest festivals, or other public gatherings. They added more tricks and more objects until Juggling Boards became its own form of entertainment.

Plate-spinning developed in a similar fashion; tricks performed using everyday objects that grew into a tradition over time. The handstand—the fundamental skill of Chinese Acrobatics— came from religious ceremonies where acrobats imitated the shape of a ding, a three-legged ceremonial vessel. They would hold a headstand, which, with its three points of contact on the ground, created a physical image that recalled the look of a ding. From there, the handstand made for a natural extension of the movement. This evolution from everyday use to entertainment happened over and over: tricks with vases developed from rituals meant to hold offerings to the gods; pole climbing acrobatics grew out of techniques used to climb trees; meteors, where acrobats spin a long rope with bowls of water, flame, or lights attached at the ends, mimicked a hunting weapon made with a flexible rattan strip attached to rocks. "Dances of Exorcism" processions warded off "plague-causing devils" while laying the cultural foundation for the lion dance—arguably China's most visible traditional performance art, at least here in the San Francisco Bay Area.

Most of these performance traditions grew independently of Western notions of the circus, and of Western influence generally (an exception being the prevalence of acts using the bicycle, which arrived in China in the late 19th century and earned the nickname "foreign horse.") As circus historian Dominique Jando writes in an essay on his website Circopedia, "Chinese acrobats can be seen in many Western circus shows; the Chinese acrobatic theater where they come from, however, is often mistakenly called 'Chinese circus' in the West. Although its artists perform acts of a similar genre and share with Western circus artists a similar background—that of the traveling fairground entertainers—their craft has evolved separately, with its own history and traditions."

As with anything that evolved over the course of a few thousand years, Chinese Acrobatics went through some high and low points. There was, of course, the aforementioned journey from commoners to court entertainment to international diplomacy; there was a Sui Dynasty performance in 610 A.D. featuring thirty thousand performers, many of them acrobats; and there was the Tang-era interest in acrobatics that led to a Chang'an court office for the Hundred Entertainments with more than ten thousand professional performers. But there were also times of war and chaos when acrobats scattered, such as the Wei, Jin, and Southern and Northern Dynasties period, which Fu Qifeng describes as a "four-hundred-year-long tangled warfare." During this period, "Hungry people swarmed the country and bodies of the starved were strewn everywhere. Under such circumstances, literature and art suffered." Acrobatic performers found work traveling as itinerant troupes of two or three, rather than in large performances for the imperial court. Still, the art form persisted. Circus, with its roots in testing the limits of human possibility, is an enduring, adaptable performance art.

The Song Dynasty's rulers disfavored acrobats and passed their opinions along to the following Yuan, Ming, and Qing dynasties, the Qing being China's final dynasty when it ended in 1911. Acrobatics, as in other periods of disfavor, remained popular with regular people. But it was often not a good living by the mid-1900s. The roving performers who populated the fairs, festivals, and permanent amusement malls of the time carried with them a whiff of the lower class. Acrobatic arts became associated with what Fu Qifeng calls "tricks of torture," or what Westerners might call sideshows. Some of these sound harmless enough—"Swallowing a Knife" and "Spitting Fire" would fit in just fine at a county fair or beach boardwalk—while others clearly had a basis in mutilation or extreme disgust factors: "Dismantling a Human Body into Eight Pieces," "Eating an Electric Bulb," or "Swallowing Five Poisonous Creatures." Common creatures for that last one were scorpions, vipers, lizards, and toads.

"In the hundred years between the Opium War and the founding of New China," Fu Qifeng writes, "traditional Chinese acrobatics met unprecedented misfortune. In the semi-feudal and semi-colonial society, under the oppression of imperialism, feudalism and bureaucrat-capitalism, the Chinese people were disaster-ridden. Folk acrobatics, which had been degraded to the lowest rung of society, suffered most. Its performers had a very insignificant social status. They were brutally exploited and unable to make ends meet."

By the time Shanghai's "Great World" amusement park opened at the end of the 19th century, acrobatics survived on an essentially exploitative business model. In a time of falling dynasties, foreign aggression, and civil wars, acrobatic performances were not top priorities for governments or everyday citizens.

Performers, trainers, organizers, and troop owners were left to fend for themselves in a difficult economy. It was this combination of laissez-fair regulation and crushing poverty that Lu Yi wandered into as a child, and that allowed him to face such bitter abuse on his way to a sustainable career.

The Communist government threw money, training space, and expertise at the country's acrobats, while discouraging and pushing aside the "tricks of torture" based in shock value. They wanted a network of classy, professional shows rooted in Chinese traditions. Like Emperor Wu of Han, they recognized the diplomatic value of Chinese Acrobatics. It was a homegrown art form that could impress the world. And impress it did.

It's worth noting here that the Foreign Languages Press, which published *Chinese Acrobatics Through the Ages* and *A Primer of Chinese Acrobatics*, the two main sources of research for this chapter, is clearly sympathetic to the Communist Party's point of view. The Press' website describes its work as "undertaking the external publicity and publishing tasks of the party and the country." A skeptical reader might question the veracity of an account written under the watch of the Communist government that claims life improved dramatically for acrobats after the Communist Party took over. But Fu Qifeng's account squares with the general circus research conducted for this book, and with the lived experiences of acrobats like Lu Yi, Xia Ke Min, Xiaohong Weng, and Jingjing Xue, who wrote about training and performing Chinese Acrobatics in the 1940s to '80s in his memoir *Shanghai Acrobat* (which features a letter of endorsement from Lu Yi at the end). The impressive accomplishments of China's acrobats, and an international reputation for excellence, also add credibility to the idea of an acrobatic resurgence during this time.

In the years following the government's reorganization of acrobatic arts, Chinese troupes traveled across Europe and Africa, stopping at times to offer workshops and training, once again using art as diplomacy. Under Lu Yi's leadership, the Nanjing Acrobatic Troupe became the first to teach Chinese Acrobatics in Australia. On the international competition circuit, Chinese acrobats became a consistent factor. Vocal mimicry specialist Sun Tai, bicycle acrobat Jin Yeqin, and pagoda bowl performer Xia Huhua all won gold medals at a World Youth Festival in 1957. Acrobat Dai Wenxia won two prizes at the Louis Merlin International Acrobatic Contests in France in 1981 for "Rolling with a Cup of Water" and, along with two teammates, "Trio Pagoda of Bowls." Chinese acrobats took home three gold medals two years later at the World Acrobatic Festival of Tomorrow in Paris. The Qian brothers of the Nanjing Acrobatic Troupe won the top prize at the famed Festival Mondial du Cirque de Demain in Paris in 1986.

Cirque du Soleil, still the standard bearer for modern circus, started hiring Chinese performers in 1994, for *Alegria*, and featured them regularly in subsequent shows, including *Saltimbanco*, *Varekai*, and others. Lu Yi, of course, left China to teach in the U.S., where he inspired generations of American acrobats who use Chinese techniques. His influence is felt so strongly here in the Bay Area that when this writer went to see *Dear San Francisco*, a semi-permanent show at Club Fugazi in the North Beach neighborhood that serves as an acrobatic love letter to the city, a performer onstage credited Lu Yi with inspiring much of the program.

Does all of this add up to the idea that Lu Yi lived through a "golden age" of Chinese Acrobatics? Maybe. Maybe not. If it was a golden age, it's one he helped build. But who is this writer to claim anytime as the golden age of Chinese Acrobatics, when it has been practiced for thousands of years? So, let's go with something less dramatic: It's a safe bet to say that if Cirque du Soleil manages to revive itself following the pandemic and bankruptcy, audiences can expect to see Chinese Acrobatics in its shows for decades to come. And the roots of that achievement can be traced back to the post-liberation era, with a sizeable chunk of credit going to Lu Yi. Meanwhile, anyone who goes to see shows like *Dear San Francisco* can expect to hear about the influence of Lu Yi for quite some time, even, perhaps, long after the man himself is gone.

ACT TWO

SEVENTEEN

'DETECTIVE' DECISIONS

The decision to leave China did not come easily. I was not one of those people who longed to live in the U.S. Despite its political problems, poverty, and other troubles, China had—eventually—led me to a pretty comfortable life. I had my home and family in a nice part of Nanjing. I had a job that I loved. You could say I had more to lose than a young man would. At the beginning of 1990, my daughters, Lu Yue and Lu Na, were in their late teens. I was fifty. That's not so old in a long life. But it's well past the age when most people want to pack up and leave their country, their culture, and their life's work. I had much to ponder on those long plane rides.

After the failed meeting with Judy Finelli at the airport, I spent only a short time in China. I ended up going back to the U.S., traveling alone again. I actually did this same round trip two or three times. I was still hoping to find the defectors, something I would not accomplish. Other than the translator, I never saw any of them again. I've heard about them working in shows, or moving to Las Vegas, or moving back to China—but it's only things I've heard, never seen. I suppose that's kind of funny. In the circus, you tend to see everyone again eventually. But these few people set out to disappear from Lu Yi's life and succeeded for decades. Maybe they should have been magicians instead of acrobats.

Not that it matters anymore. I don't have any bad feelings toward the people who defected. They did what they thought was best at the time. And that was so long ago. I could never stay angry for that many years. No one can say Lu Yi holds grudges forever.

It was on the last of those "detective" trips that I decided to stay in the U.S. I had managed to have some real meetings with Judy Finelli and other people with the Pickle Circus. They wanted me to stay and teach, to help coach acrobatics for the show. They knew about what happened in New York, and how much trouble it brought me in China. They had seen the images from Tiananmen Square on American TV, and that influenced their thinking on all matters related to China. Someone asked me, "Why do you want to go back?"

I really had to think about my answer. Why did I want to go back? Why put myself through so much trouble? I had to think about the time I spent locked away during the Cultural Revolution too. If something like that happened once, it could happen again.

While I was deliberating—alone, with no trusted advisors or friends in the U.S.—something came out in the news that forced me to deliberate even harder. A high-level official named Xu Jiatun deserted China and moved to the U.S. I knew Xu Jiatun. Not closely, we weren't friends. He was an important person I had met a few times. Xu Jiatun was the party secretary of Jiangsu Province during some of the years I ran the Nanjing Acrobatic Troupe. Nanjing is the capital of Jiangsu, so of course we ran across each other. I had no particular feelings for him. But his story troubled me.

Xu Jiatun had joined the Communist Party in the thirties and later worked in the army as a political commissar, a position that offers guidance on political thought. He held many government posts over the years. While Xu Jiatun had opposed the military crackdown on protestors in Tiananmen Square, he remained essentially loyal to the Chinese government. He believed in the Communist Party, despite its mistakes. The kind of person Americans might call "a true patriot." If someone like that felt the need to leave China, things had to be getting very complex.

The country is in chaos, I thought. *Whatever the policies, it will be a struggle. Maybe it is time for me to stay here.*

The hardest part of the decision was how it could affect my family. Wang Hong Zhu, Lu Yue, and Lu Na were all in Nanjing. If I failed to return, it could complicate things for them. We had to proceed carefully.

The Pickles helped me find an immigration lawyer—a woman named Barbara Horn—and an apartment in Berkeley. Barbara Horn helped us choose the best strategy to get my family to the U.S.—a slow one. First, she would fix it so I could stay. Then my daughters, and finally, after three long years, my wife. I don't know much about immigration law or what Barbara Horn did. I only know how trying, how bitter, it was to wait for everyone. I spoke almost no English, had no old friends to ask for advice. That Berkeley apartment was the first place where I lived alone; the first time I needed to cook my own meals.

I've said many times how much I love the circus, because that has been my life's work. But I also love my family. My career supported them financially, but they supported me emotionally. My family gave me energy. They gave me a reason to try my hardest, to stay focused. Their support allowed me to concentrate on the art form that I loved. That time without them was very difficult. It offered me a picture of a different life, one with much less joy, and a lack of purpose.

I know this time was difficult for my wife as well. Hong Zhu kept a weekly pilgrimage to the government office in Nanjing. She would walk down there and ask about her passport, and they would come up with some reason to delay it. They were angry with me for leaving, but they also wanted me to come back. Keeping her was an easy way to make my life difficult.

"Just have your husband come back," they would tell her. "Then we can let you go."

I was sad, lonely—and hungry. I could only cook basic dishes, stuff not even worth writing down. Nothing that compared to my wife's meals. (Hong Zhu is an excellent cook. She not only helped us impress people like Paul Binder and Dominique Jando, she kept our family nourished for many years. Kept us full and the kids growing. Even today, she hardly lets a visitor leave the house without a bag of dumplings.)

I felt stripped of my reputation; all of my accomplishments in China cleared away, like a theater closed for the season. All of my hard work done only to start over. Mentally, I prepared myself for a long period of effort, to face the reality that I might not achieve the same level I did in China. The feeling was not one of fear. More like acceptance, and recognition of the task ahead.

Things can never be what they were. There is nothing to do but keep moving, keep training, keep pushing. On that part, at least, I had no trouble. I started working with the Pickle Circus right away. And because acrobats train every day, I started picking up English, too. I learned from my students. Mostly just the words I needed to teach: "Handstand," "Back tuck," "Round off back handspring," "Straight arms," "More power," "Point toes." You get the idea.

Training Americans, I would soon learn, was very, very different from teaching in China. Almost like the difference between water and land, or the sun and the moon.

EIGHTEEN

A TRUE FRIEND

During those lonely, early days when I had first moved to the U.S., I made a friend. A good friend, the kind where you meet them and know instantly. One of those moments when, even though you don't understand each other's language, you understand each other. That friend was William Baer. He died in 1997, but I still think of him often.

I met William through the Pickle Circus. He was the general manager there and had a long career in the arts. He had worked as a music conductor, and as a manager for the Big Apple Circus. Our first talk happened in his office. This was at the Potrero Hill training space where I worked, at the very beginning of my time with the Pickles. Peggy Ford, a respected clown who died in 2012, introduced us. I was impressed to see that William had a small table with a Buddha statue and a metal bowl, the kind used for eating rice and temple donations. We only talked about general circus stuff, mostly using hand gestures and signing because of the language barrier, but we related to each other immediately.

William started to come and visit me in Berkeley. For a while, he seemed to be there every weekend.

Mostly we talked about circus. I had a dream to make a renowned circus school, a place with a performance company that could produce world-class acrobats. William shared that dream. We talked about our ideas for acts, shows we'd like to put together someday; storylines, costumes. We both agreed that the circus school should be very professional, with discipline and respect among teachers and students. We discussed reaching out to Asian communities to bring more students to the school. William was interested in Asian culture generally, and in Buddhism. We bonded over that too.

I had some beliefs in Buddhism. Ideas that helped guide me as a teacher and a person: be kind to people in general, try to be helpful when someone gets injured. I used to buy lottery tickets every once in a while, and I dreamed that if I won I could open a temple where young people could come and learn all the Buddhist scripts along with acrobatics. I'd put the temple in one of San Francisco's districts with a large Asian community, like Chinatown, the Sunset, or the Richmond. They could train acrobatics for free, and learn Buddhism if they wanted.

For William, though, Buddhism was something he really practiced. He would wake up very early and drive to the Sonoma Mountain Zen Center, across the Golden Gate Bridge from San Francisco, and meditate for hours. He did that kind of thing for years, all the time, training every day like a student learning the handstand. It was very important to him.

When William came to visit, we would drink tea, eat snacks, and chat. I had my Dragonwell tea and my Rainflower tea from Nanjing. William had a brand of tea he liked too. I don't remember the name but it was from Taiwan. We spent so much time together that he got to know my family. He would try Chinese foods my wife cooked and talk to my daughters about American life, as they peppered him with questions. He really helped all of us get through our major transition of leaving China and setting up here in the U.S.

Later on, William went to China to help connect acrobats there with the circus school. He was very proud to have done that, and very dedicated to our dream of high-level circus.

I got the call that William died in the afternoon. I don't remember who called, but they said he was in a car wreck. Maybe it was his wife Virginia. I don't know for sure. It was a confusing, emotional moment. The whole thing came out of nowhere; it wasn't like when someone is sick and you're waiting. William had been driving toward San Francisco from Sonoma on Highway 12. He was on his way to a rehearsal for some of his young music students. For some reason, his car veered to the left and hit a eucalyptus tree by the highway. Then another vehicle, a van, ran into his car. The driver of the van leaped out. He did some prayers with William on the side of the road, because he knew William was dying.

After the phone call, I took some wine out of my office and went to a small courtyard outside of the circus school. I took a sip of the wine, then dumped the rest in the yard. This is a Chinese tradition for when people die. A way to wish them a good trip to wherever they are going. All those ideas, those storylines and costumes—we would never be able to make them happen. Not together, anyway. Not in this life. But I would not forget our friendship. If William were here right now, I would push to continue our dream together.

Later, our whole family went to sit with William's family while he was cremated. We were all devastated. The only way our family could support theirs was to be present. The Chinese consulate sent a flower wreath as an acknowledgement of William's work with the Chinese acrobatic community. Later still, William's family gave me that metal bowl from his office, the one I had seen when we first met. I still have it in the house today.

NINETEEN

THE TORNADO IN CIRQUE DU SOLEIL

The first time I saw Cirque du Soleil was fairly early in my time here in the U.S. This was when *Saltimbanco* was touring in the United States, in the early nineties, and I had a former student, Huang Zhen, in the show. I felt a little embarrassed and a little proud at the same time. I was proud because of Huang Zhen. He performed the tornado in the Chinese pole act, and the trick was a real highlight. People leaned forward in their seats; you could see from their body language they wanted to stand up to get a better look. Huang Zhen whirled around the pole, his legs open and feet pointed, circling up higher each time he released and grabbed the pole again, using only his wrists and hands to propel him toward the top.

I had created that trick for Huang Zhen back in Nanjing. We worked on it together sometime in the eighties, maybe 1984. To me, Huang Zhen did the number one tornado on the pole. He was first and he was best. Even now, I've never seen a better tornado on the pole than Huang Zhen's. That night at *Saltimbanco*, in San Francisco, it felt wonderful to see my former student in such a great production.

So why did I also feel embarrassed? That's simple. *China could have created a show like this*, I thought, *but we did not*. China had the skill level. I've seen acrobatics from all over the world, judged circus competitions all over the world; and I still think Chinese Acrobatics is the best. But we never made a show quite like Cirque du Soleil. *Why not?*

Maybe there are other reasons, but I think it's because of the political system. Artists in China are not quite as free. The Nanjing troupe had a lot of support for developing and encouraging technical, physical circus skills. Not so much for personal expression. That's one advantage to the American system. You can say whatever you want. People are encouraged to express themselves. The Chinese methods are very good for mastering basic skills and creating high-level acrobats. But that's not the same as fostering an environment of artistic creativity. You need both to make something new and groundbreaking—which Cirque du Soleil really was at the time. It definitely helped raise the profile of circus arts here in America. I always used to dress up a bit, wearing my nice red jacket, for their shows. Other people did too. That's not to say it was fancy or stuffy. Just that people treated the show with respect. It was seen as a higher level of art. Cirque du Soleil brought that idea of circus as an important, respectable art to the United States. As a lifelong circus professional, and an immigrant to the United States, I obviously appreciated that.

I'm sure you heard about Cirque du Soleil closing all of their shows and declaring bankruptcy during the pandemic. This news brought me a lot of sadness. The company is opening some shows again now, and I hope they survive and do well. It is so hard to start a circus of that caliber; losing it would be a tragedy.

TWENTY

A TEACHING PICKLE

You may have noticed by now that I often describe acrobatics in terms of level. This is common in circus. You might say, "He is high-level." Or, "She started just okay, but now her level is good." Or, more commonly, you might go to a show and describe it later as having "low-level acrobatics." There is no particular grading system for this. It's not like a sport where judges hold up signs that read "10," or "8.5," or whatever. Someone's acrobatic prowess gets determined by their teachers, community, and audience. People in Wuqiao, Nanjing, Paris, Moscow, or San Francisco might have very different ideas about what constitutes high-level acrobatics.

I say this now because, when I started teaching in America, I had to adjust to a very different expectation of acrobatic level. I don't want to say anything bad about any particular person. I don't want people to say, "Lu Yi, you were so mean in the book." But, many years later, when someone asked me what the level of my students was when I started coaching here, I could not suppress a laugh.

"There was no level," I said. "They had no level."

This does not mean the Pickle Circus was a bad show. That's not what I am saying. In a lot of things, they were very good. They had funny clowns, talented jugglers, aerial artists, and, yes, some acrobatics. They performed mostly for family audiences outside, in public places, like parks or libraries—in San Francisco and around the Bay Area, sometimes traveling farther. And they did really well for those audiences. They made the kids laugh, the adults cheer. They built a strong reputation and tradition that people know all over the Bay Area.

The Pickle style, a friendly performance aesthetic that focused on human performers—never animals—created a unique alternative to the big-spectacle, three-ring type of shows, like the Ringling Brothers, that American circus was known for. The Pickles helped move the American circus from the old-fashioned tent-and-carnival style to the more theatrical circus that's popular today. They borrowed from the European and Russian one-ring circus traditions, the ideals of the hippie movement, and (with me!) Chinese Acrobatics to make something new, different, and unique to the Bay Area. The Pickles have even been cited as one of the influences on the founders of Cirque du Soleil. So, please, don't think I am making fun of them. I am not. But, to a serious Chinese Acrobatics person, my new students had no level. We started with the basics: handstands, stretching, simple tumbling.

Right away, I saw a huge difference between teaching in China and the United States. In China, performers start young. They need strict, consistent, disciplined training in order to excel. Many performers in China, like myself, come from poor families with few options. They might see the circus as a job, not a personal passion. The stability offered by a government company like the Nanjing Acrobatic Troupe makes for an excellent motivator. We could always choose the most talented from a wide pool of applicants. As I once told Judy Finelli, "If I have a hundred acrobats, I can break fifty of them, and it won't matter, because there will be a hundred more waiting for their spot."

But it's almost the opposite here in America. You cannot break anyone and you cannot choose the students. Everything is determined by what makes money and what individual people want to do. The Pickle Circus performers were mostly adults who chose that life; they pushed themselves to work hard. They found their own motivation. They volunteered for the intense, bitter training of acrobatics, even though their bodies were less pliable, already formed into shape by that point in life. Their passion was impressive; inspirational even. I would go home and think, *They are trying to give everything to be a better performer.* You could say we hit it off. People from very different cultures, very different traditions, who shared a strong love of circus arts.

For example, one of my more determined students, Sam Payne, was in his thirties and wanted to learn Chinese pole. That is well past retirement age for an acrobat in China. People there would say it's stupid to start pole at that age. But here he was, training every day. He worked without being pushed, trained until his hands blistered. And on top of that, he still had to pay for rent and lessons. Sam had a few jobs; he would finish an office shift, then come and train Chinese pole with me afterwards. I was impressed. I could see that his training was bitter too, in its own way.

Sam met his future wife, Sandra Feusi, at the school. They ended up joining Cirque du Soleil together, and later made a great duo pole act called "Vertical Tango." They took the act all over the world and won medals at several festivals, including the Festival Mondial du Cirque de Demain in Paris. You might have seen them here in San Francisco at Teatro Zinzanni, a tent-dinner show that used to be on the Embarcadero.

To work with the kind of students I encountered here in America, I had to reframe my thinking. Everyone starts from zero in China. They spend years working on basic skills. But I can't tell an American adult to travel back through time and use their earliest days on one-hour handstands. I can't change the shape of their bones, even if they're willing to do every stretching exercise. I had to work with the materials in front of me.

Over time, I got better at focusing on each specific person. I looked at someone's physique, thought about their background and size, and picked skills based on that. As much as I could, I encouraged people to practice handstands and stretching. Americans, in general, don't like stretching—even the kids. So I would try to find specific stretches that would help people complete a trick, to show them the benefits of being flexible. For example: if your shoulders are too tight, it's very difficult to do a back handspring. But do enough backbends, and this trick becomes much, much easier. I also tried to think strategically about the skills that were lacking in America, to make our show more unique. Hoop diving and tumbling came to mind.

The Pickle performers improved quite a lot. They had some good, dedicated people: John Gilkey, a clown and juggler, worked on his acrobatics and later joined Cirque du Soleil as a character actor. Diane Wasnak and Jeff Raz were very funny clown performers. They worked with me on doubles tricks, and both have had long, distinguished performance careers. (If you are enjoying this story, you should check out Jeff Raz's book, *The Secret Life of Clowns*). The Pickles started to perform in more indoor spaces, theaters and such, and to travel more. We went around California, to Oregon, to Alaska, and to Japan. We hired performers from China to raise the acrobatic level. There was even a run at the Kennedy Center in Washington, D.C. Around the Christmas holidays, the Pickles held an annual extravaganza in San Francisco at the Palace of Fine Arts. This was a great event, because it presented the circus as a more serious art form. People dressed up; important donors hobnobbed with local VIPs at the after-party; and everything happened in one of the city's better-known venues. It was similar to the type of gala that a big theater or ballet company might have, which was quite unusual for an American circus at that time.

As much as I enjoyed working with the Pickles, I never quite understood the name. And I know I'm not alone. We ran into a funny bit of misunderstanding during the Japan performances in 1994. Jeff Raz and Diane Wasnak were in that show, doing their "Pino and Razz" clown act. Jeff Raz is a tall person—with a wide, friendly face and black curly hair—so tall he would have to lean down to whisper something to me. Between shows, he informed me that some people in the local audience were confused by the name Pickle.

"They think it means condom," he said. Not exactly the image you want people to have of your circus.

I did suggest changing the name at one point. I thought we should pick a name that sounded more professional, and some of the performers from China agreed with me. But, of course, that didn't go through because there was a tradition. People in the Bay Area know the Pickles. They love the Pickles. The name is part of their quirky heritage. You see the Pickle on the poster; you go to the show for the "Big Juggle" and the wire-walker in a gorilla costume. Professionalism is not the only point.

Also, the Pickles had bigger things to worry about than the name.

TWENTY-ONE

THE GYM WHERE IT HAPPENED

The Pickle Family Circus never had much money. That is not a unique situation in America. Government support for circus arts is much lower than in China. I had gotten used to having resources after all those years with the Nanjing Acrobatic Troupe. In San Francisco, I had to get used to not having them. The first training space I used with the Pickles was an old warehouse in Potrero Hill. No heating, no air-conditioning, little equipment. In that way, it harkened back to the old Pan Yin days in Shanghai.

The Pickles were quite good at making art from meager materials. Instead of mats, we had carpet picked up from the streets. People in the Potrero Hill neighborhood seemed to like the circus, so the Pickles would go around and gather old, unneeded stuff to use in the warehouse. Everything seemed very casual in that way. Maybe too casual for a business. Not long after I started, the circus went bankrupt.

I didn't have much to do with the business side of the Pickles. I was still learning English and focused on acrobatics. But I know they made at least one very smart decision.

Before the money problems became insurmountable, the circus separated itself from its public training program. The Pickles, always looking to spread their love of circus arts, had started a school in 1984. The San Francisco School of Circus Arts aimed to bring high-level circus instruction to all. Aspiring professionals, young kids, regular folks with regular jobs: if you could pay the fee (and sometimes even if you couldn't), you could take the classes. Unsurprisingly, this was a more sustainable operation than a community circus. It is very hard to keep a circus company going from shows alone in America— a fact I would face more than once during my decades of working here.

With the circus in so much financial trouble, I ended up teaching at the school more. The Pickles went through a lot of complicated maneuvers to buy the company out of bankruptcy. At some point they renamed it the New Pickle Circus. Eventually, the San Francisco School of Circus Arts purchased the rights to the Pickle name. It was almost like a family, with ups, downs, and in-betweens, but always together: the Pickles made the school; the school went on to buy the Pickles. Owning an innovative circus gave the school "stage cred"; and the success of the school added to the Pickles' legacy. Not bad for a circus that some people confused with a condom!

Around this time, we started a pre-professional program for young people. At first it was called San Francisco Circus Arts. That seemed too long, so we changed it to San Francisco Circus, then later we called it Youth Circus or San Francisco Youth

Circus. Some of my most talented, most successful American students came from that program.

Some six months after I started, the training headquarters moved across town. The new space was still cold, but better equipped. It was in an old high school gym on Frederick Street, across the street from Kezar Stadium, where the San Francisco 49ers once played, and a few blocks from the Haight-Ashbury neighborhood. This became the permanent home of the San Francisco School of Circus Arts, which later changed its name to Circus Center, and is still there, in the same gym, today. You should go and visit. Tell them you read Lu Yi's book and you want to see where he worked all those years.

If the desk person is in a good mood, they might take you to the gym. The doors are straight ahead, just a few feet from the public entrance of the Circus Center. In my day, they opened to a large, wide gym with trampolines at the back wall on the left; aerial riggings for trapeze, rope, and tissue along the right side of the room; and a short, thick blue tumbling mat covering most of the center floor. We never had a spring floor when I was teaching. I wanted the students to learn on a regular mat. If you always work on a spring floor, you come to rely on it. Then if someone removes the spring floor, tumbling gets much harder. But if you learn to tumble on a harder mat in the beginning, you build more explosive power. Then, if someone gives you a spring floor, tumbling gets much easier.

Some days, especially on weekends, there might be a flying trapeze rig set up in the gym. If you want to see where I worked, turn directly to the right, and walk maybe ten steps until you're a short ways past the red Chinese poles. That was my main spot. I spent almost three decades coaching from there. I spotted handstands, taught teeterboard, explained tumbling tricks, and pushed everyone to stretch, stretch, stretch. I gave advice about acts, and sometimes life, to anyone who asked—and a few who did not.

My students grew from children to adults. Many succeeded; some retired. People gave up, started over, and gave up again. Some got tired of my coaching and left; some came back and said I was right all along. People cried tears of joy and tears of frustration. They played music, danced, and celebrated. They sulked in the corner after long hours of bitter training. They got hurt. They got bored. Many got accepted to bigger circus schools and left, but they were forever Lu Yi students to me. Some of my students even got together and made me a T-shirt. You can probably guess what it said: "Training is Bitter," once in English, then again with Chinese characters.

I worked hard. Long hours, six days a week for many years, until my family talked me into cutting back to five. Through most of those days, I kept a tall jar of tea in my hand or perched on a handstand bench, usually Dragonwell tea or Rainflower tea from Nanjing. A small clump at the bottom of the jar, no filter, hot water up to the lid. I've been drinking tea like that since I was a child. I kept the jar closed and would open it occasionally for a sip, often between rounds of handstand spotting. It would be impossible to count how many gallons of tea I sipped standing there in the gym, next to my benches.

After seeing the gym, you might be tempted to ask about my office. Don't bother. It was in a space off to the side of what we called the theater, a smaller room the school uses for some classes and small performances. The office was nothing but simple white walls, a few photos, and two desks. The other desk was for Xia Ke Min. He came over to help me teach, about two years after I started. And what a relief that was, to see Xia Ke Min arrive in the American gym. I had been worried about him staying in China. Because we were close— and I left the country—it could make things hard for him. He might be criticized, or removed from his position because of his association with me. He could be blamed for my absence and my perceived disloyalty.

Xia Ke Min and I grew up together. From Pan Yin, to the Nanjing troupe, to the Big Apple Circus; he was my most steadfast friend. If I'm doing well in life, and his circumstances are bitter, I could never be happy. I wanted us to share the same fate, to be at the same level. So once I was established here, I reached out to see if he would follow. Xia did not hesitate. He just came. We worked right next to each other in the gym, almost like when we were kids, but now as circus elders. Now, we could do things the right way. None of our students would be subjected to the cruelties of Pan Yin. None of our students would get beaten.

Later, I was able to hire another coach from China, Xiaohong Weng. He had been recruited from a gymnastic program by the Nanjing Acrobatic Troupe back in the seventies. I ran across him in Las Vegas, where he was working in a restaurant. Now, that is a perfectly fine job. I have nothing against people who work in restaurants. But it is not the ideal position for a former gymnast with decades of acrobatic expertise. Xiaohong expressed interest in becoming a coach—and he had very good English. It was an easy decision. He moved to San Francisco sometime in the mid- to late-nineties and the three of us held steady as the main Chinese Acrobatics coaches at the school for twenty years. Xia retired a few years after me, and after that, Xiaohong retired as well. Xia lives close to me still, in the East Bay. Xiaohong moved to Taiwan.

Many people look forward to retirement. I was not one of them. I loved teaching, loved working, loved my students, and, above all, loved acrobatics. I felt lucky to be able to share the art form. Young, adult, professional, recreational, pre-professional, even the ones who were just curious: I found joy in teaching them all. I tried to help them meet their goals, whatever those goals might be. That was my job. I had so many students over the years, it's hard to mention names or any specific person. I don't want anyone to feel left out. I don't want anyone to say, "Lu Yi didn't mention me in the book, he must not have loved me." That statement could never be true. I loved every student. But people say you need stories for a book. That's part of the marketing.

So I will try to recall a few moments with my many, many American students.

TWENTY-TWO

TEETERBOARD TALES

It was always the glasses.

So much trouble with the glasses. They fell off my face all the time. Some days, they seemed to fall constantly. You know how little things seem big when they keep happening? For me, the glasses were one of the most frustrating aspects of my new coaching life.

Back in China, I rarely had to spot people. My job was to look at the big picture, as overall director of acrobatics. I told the coaches how to spot people; told them how to train people; told people what they got wrong on a trick; told them which acts to work toward; told them where to be during the performance.

Teaching American beginners required a very different level of involvement. I had to get my hands underneath their hips to move their legs for a straddle press. I had to pull the safety lines for the teeterboard. I had to catch just the right spot in the student's back to propel them over in a back tuck. I had to get down on my hands and knees to straighten someone's elbows and point out how to grip the floor in a handstand. And, over and over during those things, the glasses would fall off. They would slide right down my nose onto the floor. Someone steps on them and—*crunch!* Lu Yi needs new glasses. Again.

I used to save the glasses. Like a keepsake. One time when a journalist came to the house, I showed them off. I slid the drawer open to reveal ten pairs of broken glasses—each representing a $150 replacement! My pants needed constant replacement too. The knees were always getting worn out from all that time on the floor.

Teaching children turned out to be quite different from overseeing a circus. Kids are difficult to manage. You tell them to wait, you say, "We're not ready"—but they are already running, scattered everywhere across the floor. They start doing the trick too soon, which is a great way to create accidents. Sometimes, I would close my eyes and talk to myself. *This is for the survival and reputation of the school. It will make a name for the school, and me, here in America.* Those hectic moments made me question my decision to come to the U.S. I would think, *I could have done better in China.*

We had some cultural differences around communication too. In China, you can be quite matter-of-fact with people about their body and the shape of it. American kids (and adults) reacted differently. Xia and I would sometimes tell people, "Oh, you're a little overweight," as an explanation of why certain tricks were harder. Or we might explain that the shape of their body created a challenge for specific tricks, such as how it's easier to be the base if you're stocky and the top if you're small. There are lots of examples like that in acrobatics. But the kids would get very upset and cry. They would go home to their parents and ask, "Why was I born this way?" This did not go over well with

American parents. Sometimes, they would come to the school and yell at me. That was another big difference in my new life. Back in China, I did the yelling.

Over time, I adjusted my approach. I set up quarterly meetings with the parents and discussed expectations and progress in detail. I gradually got better at communicating in an American style. I internalized what not to say in America. The three most important: "You are fat," "This looks ugly," and "You are too old." These are all definite no-nos.

It was a blessing that I got to work with so many young people. If you have no young people in your circus, then your circus has no future. The way we found students was different, but the concept was the same: people learned basics early. In China, we had selected the best people from a huge pool of applicants. In America, it was more about who wanted to train with us. But I got used to that. In some ways, it was very good. I only had students who loved the circus. In that sense, we had more in common than we did not.

Because of the different culture here, I had to think more about psychology. What motivates people, and what they are willing to do. I pushed tumbling and more endurance-based training earlier, instead of constant stretching and long handstands. I still taught all the basics, just with a little extra attention toward the things people here wanted. And, sometimes, I had to let the students make their own decisions. I told them what I thought, what I wanted, what was realistic, and then I waited.

One adult student who represented this approach was Leslie Tipton. She came and found me backstage during intermission at a Pickle show at the Palace of Fine Arts. She was thin, with long black hair and wide, excited eyes. She had just watched Zhuo

Yue perform. Zhuo Yue was a contortionist from China, one of my students who was in the show. "I want to learn that," Leslie told me.

I did not have much time, or room, to evaluate anyone backstage. Intermission is like half-time at a sporting event. Maybe it feels slow if you're in the crowd. But there is a lot going on behind the curtain. People change, make last-second adjustments, have a quick snack. Also, it's crowded. Everyone in the show has to use the same small space. But it would have been rude, and bad for business, to wave her off. In America, you have to be nice to potential students. And you always have to keep the need for funding in the back of your mind.

"Okay," I said. "Can you show me a backbend?"

Leslie sent her arms up and dropped backward right away, landing in a decent backbend. I could see she didn't have all the proper technique, but her body had good positioning. And she was flexible. I agreed to take her on and told her to visit the circus school, then turned my attention back to the show. I had no way to know if she would turn up or not. Like her training itself, everything hinged on Leslie Tipton's enthusiasm. We ended up working together for years.

At first, Leslie pushed back against my ideas. I was still teaching in a very Chinese way, and I kept focusing on handstands, handstands, handstands. By now, you know how I feel about the importance of the handstand. But Leslie got tired of them. During one of our lessons, she got very frustrated and snapped at me, "I pay you to teach me contortion, not handstands!"

Something like that would not happen in China. People there would not push back against the teacher, and the payment system is different. But here, I was responsible for my students. I could not simply explain how my methods worked. I had to convince the students they did work. This could be challenging with my limited English. I told Leslie that handstands would make everything easier, especially contortion. I explained how they would enhance the difficulty of her contortion tricks. A good handstand would open many, many possibilities.

Eventually, I must have gotten my point across, because Leslie realized I was correct, and put forth a serious, successful effort to learn a good handstand. At one point, she became a little famous in that area. She developed a strong reputation as a performer and, later, as a trainer in handstands and contortion. Leslie also managed to get into the Guinness Book of World Records. That one wasn't related to handstands. It was for stuffing herself into a suitcase.

Leslie Tipton and I ran into another cultural situation some years later. She was an established contortionist at this point, but still training with me. One day, I walked into the circus school gym and saw her across the room, working on handstands with another coach. A Russian coach who had just moved to the area and started teaching at the school. To me, this was an insult. That is simply not the Chinese way. You don't just leave your teacher with no explanation, no warning. The Chinese way is to finish learning before you move on.

I talk a lot in this book about picking up American habits. About learning American teaching methods, letting the students think creatively, encouraging them to push for what they want, not just doing what the teacher says. I have lived here for decades now. I'm a citizen who took the famous test with questions about how the American government works. I went to the ceremony where they give you your citizenship and a little American flag. In many ways, when it comes to business and how to deal with people, I approach things more like an American person. But in this case, I did not want to let go of the Chinese way.

I have no way of knowing what another teacher is doing. Maybe they approach techniques differently. Maybe I say one thing and that other coach says another. Maybe the student gets confused trying to remember two different methods. It could disrupt the flow of classes, or make their technique worse. It could even be dangerous. Acrobatics is a precise art form. One built on repetition and muscle memory. If your muscles are trying to remember totally different ways of doing the same thing, that's no good. The respectful way to switch coaches would have been to tell me. Maybe I would be hurt or disappointed, but at least I would have known. (Leslie remembers this story differently. She felt that I took sides against her in some disputes at the school, and that I stopped focusing on her development— leaving her no choice but to find another coach.)

I stayed mad at Leslie Tipton for quite some time. We did not speak to each other for weeks. But she did come back and work with me again eventually. I could not stay mad forever. That's just my nature. Once you become a Lu Yi student, you're a Lu Yi student forever, at least in my mind.

Many times, I followed the influence of both the American and the Chinese approach with my students. This was the case with Diane Wasnak, who, as far as I know, was the first woman in the western hemisphere to do men's tricks on the Chinese pole. I figured if she could learn the tricks, why not? I also taught Diane a special bicycle act. For that one, I laid out a couple of conditions: Number one, she could not practice in front of anybody. As with my "Picking Flowers" trick, no one would see this act until it worked. Number two, she could not teach the act to anyone until she was ready to stop performing it. That was the traditional approach for this number, which involves riding a bicycle backwards while kicking metal bowls onto your head. It's considered quite difficult and an honor to learn. Teaching it to an American student could have landed me in trouble back in China. But Diane Wasnak was a talented, special person, and I didn't have to worry about criticism from China so much anymore, so I went ahead.

When Diane started to make progress on the first step, which is learning to ride the bicycle backwards, she came to show me. She rode backwards in a circle three times (you have to ride in a circle so the act fits on the stage), and then asked me how many times she needed to be able to go around. I gave her a traditional answer: "One thousand."

Here is another example, one that is funnier: Youth Circus student Devin Henderson got very nervous about the teeterboard. The other kids were starting to get bigger, and he was small, so I needed him to be the top—the flyer. But when I suggested he start on the teeterboard, it was all excuses.

"Oh, my toe hurts," he would say. "I'm not ready."

Devin Henderson had followed his older brother Brad to the circus school. The whole family—well, the kids—trained together: Brad, Sadie, Devin, and Marta Henderson. They turned out to be some of my best American acrobats. For a long time, the Hendersons and another family, the Cruzes, formed the core of a "usual gang" of regulars in my Youth Circus. The Cruz kids trained together too: Raphael, who died in 2018, Francisco, and Dominic Cruz.

(Let's pause for a quick note: These two families were certainly not the only students who made up the usual gang. Many people came and went over the years. But a list of everyone would take up half the book—you would get bored, and someone would inevitably get left out. I don't want to do either of those things. So we've grabbed a few names and moved on with the show.)

Back to young Devin Henderson in the gym: A week went by. I suggested we try teeterboard again. This time, he was pacing around, still very nervous. He kept going to the bathroom. Performers do that a lot. It's especially common to have to pee right before a big show, when you feel nervous. That can be a serious logistical problem in a theater. Sometimes you don't really know how to find the bathroom, and those costumes can be hard to get on and off. Usually, the best thing to do is wait until after the show—then, a lot of times, the urge goes away.

Young Devin's turn for the teeterboard came around, and he wanted to go back to the bathroom: "I need to pee."

He left the gym. After a while, I went to check on him.

Young Devin was not peeing. He was just standing there—hiding without hiding, a blank expression on his face. He was obviously scared. I could not force Devin, who was only about nine years old, to do the teeterboard. In America, the students and their parents decide a lot, sometimes even more than the coach. But I knew, with the proper effort, Devin had the potential to be very good at teeterboard. And working through nerves is a big part of being a performer. What could I say to convince him? I went with the direct approach.

"You're nervous. Just get over it," I told him. "Give it a chance."

I headed back downstairs. Sure enough, he followed a few

130

minutes later. Devin made the decision to try the teeterboard on his own.

The first trick you practice on the teeterboard is a straight jump, in a safety belt with two thin ropes attached. What we call "in lines." It's very safe, especially with a light person. The ropes run up to wheeled pulleys rigged from the ceiling, and come back down to my hands. I wear gloves, left hand holding on near my waist, right hand raised a bit past eye level with my palm turned outward, almost like I'm checking a watch. From there, I could hold young Devin Henderson in midair if I needed to.

Just like I would have instructed someone back in China in my *On Teeterboard* pamphlet, Devin held a steady forward gaze, and slapped his thighs with straight arms to indicate he was ready for his partner to jump on the other end of the board. He shot up for the first time. And he landed pretty well. Not beautiful, but good enough.

Later, Devin Henderson became very good at teeterboard. Also at tumbling, hoop diving, pole climbing, and other things. He went on to work with a well-regarded company called 7 Fingers, co-founded with two veterans of the Pickle Circus, Gypsy Snider and Shana Carroll; he toured with Cirque du Soleil; and, eventually, he joined former Youth Circus members Maya Kesselman and Dominic Cruz to start a circus company called Back Pocket.

But before all of that happened, Devin Henderson did something else—another milestone shared by several of my Youth Circus usual gang. He left. He left San Francisco to train at a more professional circus school. The kind of place that teaches theater, acting, dance, and a bit about the business of circus. Over and over, my best students left for other schools. This bothered me. I wanted to build something here in America that would rival the skills and talents of China. Something Americans could compare to Cirque du Soleil. Something people would know about around the world.

I wanted to make Circus Center the school people came to from other places; not the one they left. That was my American dream.

TWENTY-THREE

WATCHING YOUR CHILDREN LEAVE

Most of the students who left went to the École Nationale de Cirque, the national circus school in Montreal, Canada. People call it ENC for short. The school is famous for turning out great performers, and for its connection to Cirque du Soleil. The Canadian circus company and its national school were connected from the start, and it still draws performers from there. (Or, at least, it still did before the 2020 coronavirus pandemic.) If your goal is to be an acrobat, there are lots of places in the world to train. But if what you really want is to join Cirque du Soleil, ENC might be the best option, if you can get in. The school can be quite selective. It mirrors China in that regard. We see this over and over in circus—countries that support the art form produce high-level performers, companies, schools, and institutions. Countries that don't support the art form produce things at a lower level.

Raphael and Francisco Cruz and Brad Henderson were some of my first students to head to ENC. This was sometime in the early 2000s. Around the same time they made an exciting Chinese pole number with good, high-energy, hip-hop beats. I guess it worked. People at the Circus Center were excited when they got into ENC. I was excited too. I was happy for my students' future, and proud of their accomplishment. But something in my face must have betrayed disappointment to see them go. As people were celebrating the news, a juggler at the school named Beejay Joyer, who started in acrobatics with the Youth Circus but switched to juggling after hurting his wrist, came over to me on the walk from the gym to my office. He put a hand on my shoulder.

"At least you still have Devin," he said, meaning young Devin Henderson. "He's the best, anyway."

I was sad again a few years later, when Devin Henderson was accepted at ENC. He was followed by several others. One by one, the Youth Circus gang left my school for that other one: Marta Henderson, Dominic Cruz, Philip Rosenberg, Joren Dawson, and so on down the list. Maya Kesselman went to L'Ecole Superieure des Arts du Cirque, or ESAC, a circus school in Belgium. Going to a school other than the famed ENC did not slow her down. She won a gold medal at the Festival Mondial du Cirque de Demain in Paris, and went on to perform with Cirque du Soleil, among other accomplishments.

Watching the Youth Circus gang leave, I felt like an abandoned parent. Like you raised your son, and then your son went to live with someone else. These other schools became their second life. I didn't blame the kids for leaving. I just wished they had no need to; I wished that conditions were better here. That an ambitious student had more options in San Francisco, and the U.S. in general. I tried to raise the level of the San Francisco school to match places like ENC, but that presented insurmountable challenges. The ambitious students had no choice. I understood.

Some people might ask why. "Why can't Lu Yi make this school better, more professional?"

The simple answer is money. The schools in Canada and Europe get funding and support from the government and from the people. Regular people respect the circus as a serious art form in Europe, China, and Russia. Not so much in the U.S. Most people here don't think of circus quite like they do ballet, or theater. Maybe that is getting better now, I hope. But at the Circus Center, you always had to have money in the back of your mind. To think about how much the show cost, how the school is doing financially. Also, back then, the school could be a little disorganized.

Successful organizations tend to have a core, an important person to push decisions. In China, in the Nanjing Acrobatic Troupe, that person was me. I could not do that here. The culture was different, the business was different—the language was different. My best contribution was to focus on the arts side. I did not have the expertise to make major decisions about the direction of the school, or to implement them. Those decisions fell to the administrators, the executive director, the board of directors. They were the leaders, and the Circus Center went through a lot of them over the years. At times, it was unclear which direction the school wanted to turn.

Someone would make a decision; then a short time later someone else would make a change to that decision; and then another short time later someone else would make a change to the changed decision. People came and went, and came back again. Personal relationships got complicated, and some people seemed to have their own agendas. Maybe they wanted to spin off and make their own training facilities, or their own name. I thought the school needed to make some central decisions and stick to them. When I pushed for that, people would say "yes" to the front of my head and "no" to the back of it.

In the meeting, maybe they would say it's a good plan. But later, when I'm not around: "This is impossible. We don't have the money." I would rather people be honest. Just tell me, "We can't afford it," or, "That's not practical," to my face.

None of this is to suggest that Circus Center was a failure. Not even close. We did a lot with what we had. Jeff Raz, from the Pickles, started a program called the Clown Conservatory that trained a whole generation of performers in American- and Pickle-style clowning. As I mentioned at the very beginning, we took some of those clowns to China, introducing the Clown Conservatory's work to Chinese performers. That idea came from an offhand conversation I had once. A man from a circus in Italy told me he didn't think Chinese clowns were funny. He said people are born to be funny. I disagreed, using a joke: "Well, then maybe we should bring some foreign people over to marry some Chinese people and that will produce some funny clowns." I was kidding about the marriage part, but the rest of the idea stuck with me. As I worked more with the Pickles and the Circus Center's clown program, it sounded better and better.

For the first session, in 2008, we sent a mix of professional clowns, teachers, and students from the Clown Conservatory for a month-long workshop hosted by the Nanjing Acrobatic Troupe, which we called the Nanjing Clown Workshop. Famed Bay Area clown Joan Mankin, who died in 2015, led the classes, along with Jeff Raz and clown students Jonah Katz—one of my Youth Circus gang—and Caroline "Linie" Orrick. They taught physical humor, character work, costumes, make up, and the general, free-form playfulness that helps American clowns connect with an audience. I went toward the end of the workshop period, and we put together a show called *Journey to Nanjing*. It mixed Western-style clowning and humor with dance and Chinese Acrobatics for a simple story about an American named Jonah, played by our Jonah, who gets lost in Nanjing.

The workshop was attended by magicians, acrobats, and performers from all over China, including Beijing, Wuhan, Yinchuan, Anhui and Taiyuan. Officials from the national and regional arts and culture departments across China came as well, making for an exciting moment in my career. I had left China under difficult circumstances, worried about how my departure would affect my friends, family, and acrobatic troupe. Now, I was welcomed back by my old colleagues, and could see the continuation of my beloved Chinese Acrobatic tradition up close.

For the people in China, I could point with pride to my talented, funny, American clown friends. And for the Americans, I could show them the high acrobatic standards I helped create in China. It gave me a chance to "marry" my Chinese family with my American family—and it worked! We "produced" some funny clowns. Some years after the workshop, we also took clowns from the school to the Wuqiao International Circus Festival. If my health had held up better, I would have pushed more cross-cultural projects like that.

Also in 2008, the United States Synchronized Swimming team trained at the school to prepare for the Beijing Olympics. They came around once a week for a couple of months. I worked with them on partner acrobatics, and developing more power. Their coaches wanted the women to learn how to execute the flips, extensions, twists, and tricks they performed in the pool on the floor, to make the team more adaptable, and to help them understand the mechanics of the movements. This was a really wonderful group. Hard-working and creative, with beautiful tricks and good ideas. I especially enjoyed working with them. Of course, they spent most of their time at their own gym, training in the water. But it was a great honor to offer some acrobatic knowledge to a U.S. Olympic team.

Dominique Jando, who had come to Nanjing with Paul Binder back in the eighties on that Big Apple Circus expedition, worked with Circus Center for a time, focusing on the overall vision of the school. Elena Panova, an excellent swinging trapeze artist from Russia who married Dominique Jando, moved to the Bay Area then too, and taught an aerial arts program. My Youth Circus churned out many talented acrobats, and I'm very, very proud of all of them. So it's fair to say that our school had most of the elements it needed to be truly professional—maybe everything besides money. But we never quite managed to put them all together, and that still makes me sad. It is one dream I could not accomplish.

Part of what makes this so disappointing is that we had a system that really worked for skills training. Business people might call it "proof of concept." When *Traces*, an intimate, theatrical show by 7 Fingers, came through San Francisco, it had a cast of five people—and four of them were from my Youth Circus. *Traces* is a show that requires a lot of its performers. They have to move well, almost like dancers, and express themselves, almost like actors. They have to do a lot of acrobatics: tumbling, pole, handstands, a hoop-diving finale. In a lot of ways, it's harder to make an entire show with fewer people. You can't rely on spectacle or costumes or big group numbers. It takes some really talented people.

Traces played at the Palace of Fine Arts. After the show, I ran into someone from Cirque du Soleil who commented on how rare it is to find such versatile performers.

"At Cirque du Soleil," he told me, "it's hard to find five people to do a whole show."

That stuck in my head. I was obviously proud that my students could pull off such a difficult performance. But, at the same time, it made me sad that they had to leave to fulfill their potential. *They should have stayed here*, I thought. *There should be a circus here that would give them opportunities to perform.*

Later, I decided to make one: Acrosanct. It would be like 7 Fingers for San Francisco. Or, at least, that was the idea. I can't say it happened quite like any of us hoped.

MUCH MORE THAN A BREAK

I first noticed the symptoms in Canada. Out of nowhere, I had trouble walking. That very simple movement, one leg in front of the other, suddenly became very complex. Very difficult and confusing. All my life, I maintained a strict sense of control and discipline over my body—even in my seventies, I made a point to do five handstands a day. To have that control leave so suddenly was quite disorienting, like my mind and body got mixed up at the same time.

I had gone to Montreal for the American Circus Educators conference in 2014, an event put on by the American Youth Circus Organization, or AYCO. Cirque du Soleil had invited AYCO to hold the event at the National Circus School. I was set to receive a teacher's award from AYCO and to watch some of my old students perform as part of their graduation from ENC. My strange walking discombobulation happened on the way to the show.

Later, during the performance, I noticed I had trouble staying in one position. I could not sit too long; I could not stand too long; I could not walk too long. It was a very weird and disturbing feeling. I did not understand what was happening, so I told myself what made sense. I told myself what I think anyone in my position would have said. What I wanted to hear.

I am just tired, I thought. *I need to take a break.*

A break. Unfortunately, I needed much more than that.

We did not find out what was actually wrong for a while: Parkinson's disease. The National Institute on Aging calls it "a brain disorder that leads to shaking, stiffness, and difficulty with walking, balance, and coordination." When I received this diagnosis, I did not even know what it meant, and, at first, I did not take it seriously. I was used to pain; my back, my knees, my wrists. I had spent my life jumping, tumbling, standing on my hands, catching Xia Ke Min on my head. Pain seemed normal, almost predictable. But a loss of control? That seemed vague. Difficult to believe. Over time, it made me sad and sluggish. It became hard to say where one health problem ended and another began. Either way, the time had come to make some changes. I could only do so much.

I decided to step back from daily teaching to focus on the new company, Acrosanct. The Circus Center had a party for me on my last day.

They held the party in the theater, that room on the other side of the building from the gym where the school hosted shows sometimes. This room is much smaller than the gym, and back then it had no real theater equipment. The "stage" was a raised section of the floor left over from the building's days as a high-school gym. The main floor in the theater stayed covered by the same type of thick, blue tumbling mats as the ones in the gym. For my party, they brought in portable tables covered with food, and everyone gathered together. Teachers, administrators, long-time students. Of course I had to give a speech.

At this point, I had been teaching in the U.S. for about twenty-five years. That's long enough that it was pretty hard to say goodbye. To think of Xia and Xiaohong teaching alongside me for so many years. People from the Pickles, like Judy Finelli and Wendy Parkman, who helped me get started; Jeff Raz, his American clown style and good humor; Patrick Osbon, who served as the school's executive director for many years; all of my Youth Circus gang. And you can't forget everyone in the office, the people who take the phone calls and deposit the money and work on the budget. They make our circus possible.

I thanked everyone. I told them how much I appreciated their love, support, and respect over so many years. I told them how I wanted the school and Acrosanct to work together; similar to how Cirque du Soleil and ENC help each other. I told them how I hoped this wasn't so much of a goodbye as a see-you-around. And I cried. Right there in front of the whole school, with real tears. After the party, I went home, for the last time as artistic director of the Circus Center.

This chapter would end better with a happy story, or a good moral. A scene where I look out the car window on the Bay Bridge, heading back to Berkeley with a sense of accomplishment and closure. A moment of reflection; relief that I would soon face a much easier workload. But that's not how it went. Looking out that car window, there was only sadness. I wanted to work. I did not want to retire, or slow down, or step back, or semi-retire, or choose to only focus on one thing—or anything like that. My health forced me.

If there was any consolation, it was Acrosanct. But even that would prove to be a short-lived source of optimism.

TWENTY-FIVE

MY ENCORE: ACROSANCT

Was it good enough for a final show? Would I have changed things, if I'd realized Acrosanct was my last professional production? Maybe, but not much. I spent my life working to make every show the best it could be; there's no reason to think I gave up at the end. I did not get my fingers stomped on, my head beaten with a stick, and my fingers frozen from spinning plates outside in the cold to get lazy in America. We worked hard on Acrosanct, even if the company did not continue the way I hoped.

The plan was grand. A major performance company for San Francisco, with its own space where the performers could live and train full-time. Giving the performers a place to live solved a crucial problem: San Francisco is so expensive that people spend tons of time and energy just to find a pillow and a bed. They work too much to afford the rent, or they live far away and waste hours on a long, boring commute. That kind of stuff drains your creativity. It's like pulling the stopper out of a bathtub.

The warehouse seemed perfect, and wasn't far from where I used to teach the Pickles. It was a bit farther east, where the city meets the bay water, and a bit south, in an area that used to be rundown but was getting more expensive and fancy every year. Ayla and Jory Bell, adults with business experience who trained in acrobatics with me at the circus school, were renting the space already. They were dating then and are married now. Ayla had come to the school a few years earlier to study, but got deeply involved in the administrative decision-making when the school found itself in serious financial trouble—trouble so bad it considered shutting down. For a while, Ayla volunteered as executive director. We came to respect each other. She trusted my artistic and acrobatic knowledge, and I trusted her business sense. I wanted to start a new circus for San Francisco, and so did she. Acrosanct worked for both of us. It was a training program for aspiring acrobats, and a professional company for working performers.

Brad Henderson from my Youth Circus gang joined as acrobatic coach. He had a very flashy job title: chief acrobatics officer. Mine sounded dull by comparison, the same one I had at Circus Center—artistic director. Having Brad Henderson there was crucial, because I could trust his acrobatic technique. I had a lot of pain, health problems, and doctor visits. I couldn't work as much as before, couldn't spot people so often, or pull lines the way I used to. Brad Henderson understood my approach to training. I could leave him with wood and come back to find a cabinet. Figuratively, that is. I don't know if he can actually make a cabinet. Other folks from my Youth Circus gang came and helped out too, if Brad needed to take a contract and I couldn't teach.

The new company had logistical troubles from the start. San Francisco can be very strict about permits, zoning, remodeling things, and the type of buildings people can live in. We wanted to make some changes, but there was some kind of permit problem with a loft in the top of the warehouse where Jory and Ayla stayed. They ended up having to tear the whole thing down. And, of course, there wasn't enough financial backing for all the things I wanted. My ambitions and high hopes outweighed the company's bank accounts. In the end, we only made one professional show.

I would have liked to keep going. I did not think of our show as my final production. Everyone wanted to make more. But my health got too poor. The pain in my back worsened. Some days, I would lie down on my back with an equipment belt, the kind we use to keep people in safety lines, and toss it around the base of a pole, gripping the belt on each side. Then, Brad would pull my legs. The belt was easier to hold on to than the pole, and as it grew taut this would lengthen my body into a gentle stretch that offered a small amount of relief.

At least we can say our one show was pretty good. It was called *This is Acrosanct*, and had a very simple theme about people coming to San Francisco to learn to work together for a circus. Basically, the story of the training space and the new company. Our director for the show was Jaron Hollander, who has lots of experience in theater. The show had a good mix of dance, theater, and a modern circus style, with some very nice acrobatics. The opening charivari was set to very high-energy modern electronic music, and ended with a four-high. Brad Henderson did the "tornado" on the Chinese pole, the move I created with Huang Zhen that made it into Cirque du Soleil's *Saltimbanco*. The teeterboard number had a series of high jumps and tumbling that flowed together really well. It all added up to a show with real potential. The kind of show I could take back to China. That was something I had been thinking about for a while. Using American music and style, like the good beats in hip-hop music and the unique acrobatic tricks in breakdancing, and mixing it with traditional Chinese Acrobatics to create something sensational on the international circuit. *This is Acrosanct* wasn't that show yet, but it had the potential. The audience, around two hundred people, could feel it; the performers knew it; I believed it. But it wasn't to be.

At the end of *This is Acrosanct*, the curtain came down on my long career in the circus arts. Not because I wanted it to, but because life intervened: my health, the finances, everything. Reality intruded on my dream.

The crowd goes home first after a show. Then the performers and, finally, the crew. Sometimes, the last person to leave pauses for a moment before they turn off the lights. Maybe they look at the empty chairs and quiet stage, lit only by one bland house light. Maybe they think about how quiet it seems compared to earlier, when the crowd sizzled in anticipation of the show. Maybe that last person looks at the aerial rigging, the hoops stacked in the corner. Maybe they think about all the bitter training that went into creating the show. Maybe they contemplate the beauty of acrobatics. Bodies soaring through the air, flipping upside down, perched high on one arm. Maybe that person takes a breath, and gives a wistful smile before they flip off the last light.

That's when the show really ends.

TWENTY-SIX

TRAINING IS BITTER, BUT LIFE IS SWEET

The worst part of Parkinson's, by far, is the loss of my physical abilities. I spent my whole life perfecting movement, even when working to perfect that movement was terribly bitter. Working to make each muscle, each part of the body do exactly what it needed to do. Working to help others learn that level of mastery. Working to create something so amazing the audience almost couldn't believe the human body would do such things. Even after my performance years, I maintained a strict, physical discipline, always staying in the best condition possible. I could not hold a perfect, beautiful handstand after I got older, but it was good enough to stay upside down for a while. Good enough to work the muscles and the balance. Now, it's totally different. Almost the opposite. Some days, it's difficult to sit up. Sometimes I can't get out of bed. Or I do get up, but then have to go back to bed early. I lost a lot of mobility on my right side. I went from still standing on my hands to struggling to walk on my feet.

I'm afraid I can't say many nice things about retirement either. It is too boring, too slow, too empty for me. I was never one of those people content to sit on the couch and watch television. I would much rather be training, working, creating. The days now are quiet; the nights offer little besides time to think. Time to look back. Sometimes, I think about my students. I miss when I could train people. I miss working with a student and seeing them achieve something great in a short amount of time. That always gave me a great sense of pride and pleasure. Sometimes, I miss teaching so much I cry a little bit. Not really with tears running down my face, but inside. Inside my chest, my heart cries for my poor health.

My students still call me on occasion. They reach out for help with a show, or for acrobatic advice. I can't work anymore, not really, but the inquiries serve as a source of great comfort. It makes me very happy to know that people still think of Lu Yi. That my students are out there, working, training, performing, inspiring the next generation of acrobats. That they still believe my mind has something to offer, even if my body does not. I only wish I could do more.

At home, I think about my life; about the things I've done, and what I might change if I started back at the beginning. I regret some tricks. Even my most famous one.

That teeterboard head-to-head catch resulted in a lot of impact on my neck. I think it affected my muscles in a negative way. I regret doing that trick. Yes, the one you know me for the most. If I could start over, I would focus more on improving my training, thinking about the impact on the body. Making sure to build the muscles in the neck before a trick like that. Or to remember, for myself and my students, not to push for things that don't fit the person. For example: Maybe someone really wants to do contortion. But if they don't have the shape, don't have enough natural flexibility, they should really evaluate their condition with the trainer. Maybe it's better to do something else, instead of push, push, push until you harm the muscles. Maybe it's okay to let the hands be a little bit wider on the back-bend or the one-arm handstand if that fits your body type. Small adjustments like that could keep you from having too much pain later in life.

I don't have any proof that things would have turned out differently if I had used other training methods for my head-to-head trick. It's impossible to say. But when you're stuck at home, it's only natural to think about your past decisions. Sometimes I think about my life as a whole, too. It's kind of funny, but all my best times came in the middle. As a young child, I was very poor, so poor I searched the streets for scraps. When I found a bit of stability, it came under a cruel, abusive acrobatic coach. But as a teenager, I traveled the world and represented my country, which I loved. Through hard work and diligent effort I grew into a man who invented new tricks; learned to run a world-class acrobatic troupe; and coached many, many American students, watching several of them go on to great careers in the circus. Of course the man who did those things also made mistakes. But overall, I think it's a legacy to proud of. Then, in my later years, as an old man, I got very sick, and grew quite sad.

American people might say my life was shaped like a jelly sandwich on rough bread. The bitter parts happened at the beginning and the end. But the middle was pretty sweet.

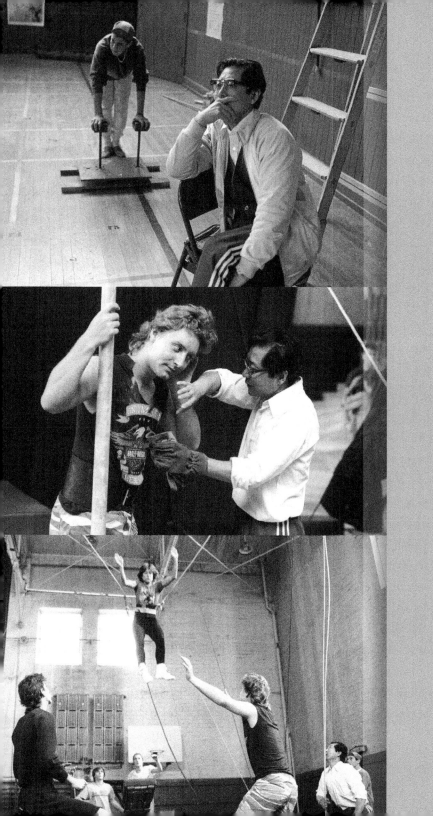

CURTAIN CALL

'FAIR BUT DEMANDING': YOUTH CIRCUS STUDENTS REMEMBER TRAINING WITH LU YI

INTERVIEWS BY DEVIN HOLT

ANSWERS EDITED FOR LENGTH AND CLARITY

⋆ *What was Lu Yi's teaching style like?*

Ron Oppenheimer, circus artist, performed with Cirque Éloize; Cirque du Soleil; Youngstage International Circus Festival: "Strict, but pushing you hard when you needed it, and knowing when to be calmer when you didn't. He wouldn't respect you unless you worked hard. And if he respected you, he would push you. But he would know when to step back a bit not to break you."

Maya Kesselman Cruz, circus artist, performed with 7 Fingers; *Dear San Francisco*; Cirque du Soleil; Circus Monti; gold medalist at Festival Mondial du Cirque de Demain;

co-founder of Back Pocket circus company: "Stern and parental. Like how a parent wants to see their child succeed, and they see themselves in their children. And then I said stern because training is bitter. It's not supposed to be easy."

Dominic Cruz, circus artist (and Maya's husband), performed with 7 Fingers; *Dear San Francisco*; Cirque du Soleil; Midnight Circus; Cirque Éloize; co-founder of Back Pocket circus company: "Fair but demanding. It's like he wasn't cold, he was warm. He was a very warm teacher, but he really delineated times between having fun and working hard. And he often equated fun with hard work. He would often laugh and make jokes. He wouldn't yell at you or whatever. He would be very encouraging.

"The only time he really would be disapproving was when you weren't prepared to work. He wouldn't teach me if I didn't have time to work. He would just totally put me on the side, which I really appreciate as an adult. He didn't cater to my child-like, underdeveloped sense of work ethic. He kept the expectations for me high enough that I would always be working toward a higher level. [...] As if I never attained mastery. I could be happy that I got a trick, but I have to know that there's always a higher level, so be humble about what you attained."

Devin Henderson, circus artist, performed with Cirque du Soleil; 7 Fingers; *Dear San Francisco*; co-founder of Back Pocket circus company: "He was a very hands-on coach. Constant spotting, stretching your pike, standing on you with his full body. He was the first one to catch you if you went flying off the teeterboard. […] When he first arrived, there may have been some difference in the way that he was taught and coached, in a more physical environment where people got hit with sticks or on the back of the neck. I think he had to tone it down a bit for Western society. There were times he would come up behind you and hit you with his shoe. But you kind of knew it was coming, because you probably already knew you were up to no good."

✕ *What was Lu Yi's reaction when you did something incorrectly?*

Maya Kesselman Cruz: "He would make funny sounds, or make a grunt, or a sound of astonishment; upset astonishment. Or just be like, 'The girl,' and shake his head. But he could give you a look and you know you did something wrong."

Dominic Cruz: "He would say, 'It's okay. Just keep trying. It's okay, no problem, just keep trying. You can do it. More round off. Training is bitter. You can do it.' He would also say, 'Turn your hand this way, look at the floor,' all the technical things. But so often I remember him being like, 'Don't worry about it. That's what training is for. What you're trying to do is hard.'"

Maya Kesselman Cruz: "There was a lot of like, 'Okay this is what you need to fix. If you just look up instead of looking down in this move, it's gonna be better.' And then you try that and it works. Just the tiniest little detail in the world and

155

it makes a difference. Actually, to this day, he does that. He came to see us at Club Fugazi (where *Dear San Francisco* plays in San Francisco). He told me he was still fixing my round off. He was like, 'Your ankles are weak, you need to be strong.' In the state that he's in now, like he's still my teacher after all these years. He still had interest in making me better."

Dominic Cruz: "I feel like he was really calculating with my training. At one point he was having me do, like, a hundred round offs a day. So many round offs. He'd leave and come back and be like, 'Show me a round off.' He'd leave and come back and change something. Then he'd have me get the mats out, and have Xiaohong hold the hoops. And he'd be like, 'Do four hoops now.' And then it worked out. He'd get the round off right and then I could do it."

⋆ *What about when you got something right?*

Or Oppenheimer, systems engineer at software company Carbon (and Ron's sister): "He would always have a big grin on his face when you succeeded at something, especially if you had been working on it for a long time. Usually followed up by corrections and how to do it better."

Maya Kesselman Cruz: "His posture would change; like a celebratory posture. It wasn't so much in his words as it was about the physical way he responded to us, his body language. He was a performer, after all, so he didn't need to use his words to get his point across."

Devin Henderson: "He had these hardware gardening gloves that he used for spotting and pulling lines. If you did the trick correctly, once you got down from the pole or teeterboard or whatever, he would take one of the gloves off and show you his hand and you'd get a high-five and that was approval. You knew you did it right."

Ron Oppenheimer: "If I did a good job at something he would immediately be thinking like, 'Oh you're ready for the next steps.' So he would throw everything I did wrong about it. Like, 'Okay, it's working, let's move on.' When I was good, he would tell me it was bad. And when it was bad, he would tell me it was good, so I wouldn't feel bad about myself. So, good old manipulation, in the best way possible."

✳ *What is it about training with Lu Yi that seems to inspire people so much?*

Maya Kesselman Cruz: "I think it might be the sense that you are responsible for your success, but I'm here for help. Like, 'I'm here to help you but you have to put in the work.' I think, especially as a child, I could celebrate my successes with him—but I knew they were my own, because I was expected to show up and do the work."

Ron Oppenheimer: "I think it's because, even in the way he looks at things, you can tell how much knowledge and history he has. So when he sees the potential for something to be great, you can see that, and you immediately want to nurture it and make it better."

Or Oppenheimer: "Since I did train at a few other gyms, what I really appreciated about Lu Yi's Youth Circus as opposed to other ones, was it focused on very high-quality circus. Whatever you do, do it well. Other gyms focused on performances or putting together your act. That wasn't the emphasis of the program. The emphasis was on training and building your skills as opposed to showing off that training. I really appreciated that kind of focus. Because if you have a good basis, then you can do anything you want later on."

Joren Dawson, artist and producer, performed with Gravity and Other Myths; Edinburgh International Festival; Club Swizzle: "One of the most incredible things about Circus Center and Lu Yi is that most people, when they do an after school activity, they don't have the drive to turn that into their life. But everywhere I go in the world performing circus shows, everyone knows San Francisco acrobats. And that just doesn't really exist in many things. It's pretty unlikely that you'd take an after school kids class in San Francisco and they'd almost all dedicate their life to that activity. [...] There's this small, little building, a place where people go and do some circus skills, and from there they take over the world."

✳ *What sort of career do you think you would have if Lu Yi had never come to the circus school?*

Dominic Cruz: "Oh my god...I'd either probably be a musician or a dentist. I'd probably follow one of my parents. I was such a kid who idolized people, and I definitely idolized my parents. And I was in my mom's choir my whole life. I hung out at my dad's (dental practice) office a whole lot."

Or Oppenheimer: "I didn't go into circus in the end. Unlike my brother, who at age nine already knew he wanted to go to Circus Center, I knew pretty early on that wasn't what I wanted.

"Something about now as an adult working as an engineer at a tech company—I know that's a very stereotypical thing for the Bay Area—what I define as exercising is very different than everyone else. I don't need a gym. I just need a mat. Kind of the same stuff we did in class to warm up, I'll do to work out. Even in my little apartment I'll do kicks to warm up. Even though I'm not a professional, it's still good exercise, having that routine."

Ron Oppenheimer: "I grew up doing gymnastics, grew up doing Splash Circus (in Emeryville). So I might be doing very different disciplines because I wouldn't have been exposed to Chinese pole, but I would still be very much doing circus. Maybe it would have made me less likely to succeed. But I think I still could have done it because I was very headstrong. But if not, I probably would have been a software engineer or in Silicon Valley. That was always the backup plan."

Maya Kesselman Cruz: *Long pause follows the question.* "I have no idea. If Lu Yi had not come to the...well, he was the circus school. So there would be no Youth Circus without him. And he brought Xiaohong and Xia, so there would be no teachers to teach us Chinese Acrobatics. So, no teachers, no careers. *Well, what do you think you would be doing, in that case?* I got asked this by an interviewer for Fugazi the other day. Super thrown off by this question. I've always done circus. It's hard to imagine. In an alternate reality, a lot of things might have been different. I'd like to think that I would have been determined to be disciplined enough to have gone and done something else. But I have no idea. I learned a lot of my discipline from circus, so, I don't know."

Joren Dawson: "I wouldn't be doing circus that's for sure. I now run another arts company that makes big installation art, and I don't think I would have created that either. It's all very interconnected. The company my wife (Jascha Boyce, co-founder of Gravity and Other Myths) runs in Australia potentially wouldn't have existed without the influence of *Traces*. And would *Traces* exist without the influence of Lu Yi? I think you could harken back to, if Lu Yi hadn't taught at Circus Center, would this Australian company be doing a show opening the Edinburgh Festival? I don't think so. [...] The guy changed a lot of lives."

EPILOGUE:
'XIÈXIE NÎ': LU YI OFFERS
ONE MORE LESSON

BY DEVIN HOLT

In some ways, it felt like a normal training day—at least for the kids-turned-adults who had spent so much of their lives in the San Francisco Circus Center's Youth Circus program. The acrobatic masterclass given by Lu Yi and Xiaohong Weng in August 2021 followed the standard progression: line up in height order; acknowledge the teachers; kicks in lines on the mats; followed by handstand rolls, handstand hops, cartwheels, round offs, round off back handsprings, round off back tucks, round off back handspring back tuck, round off with *two* back handsprings and a back tuck—and so on down the line as far as the participants' skill levels allowed. But for anyone familiar enough with this scene to know that hoop diving would follow, some obvious, important differences emerged.

First and foremost: Lu Yi, always known for his dedication to physical pursuits, for continuing to practice his handstand decades past the age when most acrobats retire, now sat in a wheelchair. His arms moved little; his voice, rarely loud to begin with, stayed much quieter than an old student would remember, difficult to hear even through the microphone given to him by the class organizers. Also a bit odd, for a training day, was the presence of an audience. Some fifty to seventy-five people assembled in the upper bleacher seats of the Circus Center's large gym to watch this final hurrah between Master Trainer Lu Yi and a sampling of the students he inspired. To make matters even weirder, there was the near-universal use of that pandemic fashion accessory: the mask. Everyone wore them: the crowd, Circus Center Artistic Director Felicity Hesed, all-around Bay Area clown legend Jeff Raz, and the Pickle Circus member who convinced Lu Yi to come to America, Judy Finelli. Even the acrobats wore masks, and they did not take them off for training. It was a shout-out to the past about the influence of Lu Yi, and a postcard to the future about the nagging inconveniences and behavioral adjustments required to make art in a stubborn, lingering pandemic.

"It was a quite special and emotional day," Maya Kesselman Cruz said. "In a really weird time."

The idea for the masterclass came from Felicity Hesed. She knew that Xiaohong planned to move to Taiwan at the end of the year. The event would acknowledge his service to the school, and Lu Yi's pioneering role in cementing Chinese Acrobatics as the foundational art of the Circus Center.

"I really wanted people to get a taste from the class of the fundamentals of Chinese Acrobatics, as well as a sense of the heights to which it can reach," Hesed said in an email. "I wanted them to see the master instructors at work."

Before things started, Hesed introduced the acrobats as a

mix of former students and current cast members of *Dear San Francisco*. Then she passed things over to Jeff Raz, who encouraged the crowd to ponder the significance of the moment for a planned Q-and-A.

"As you're watching, I would love it if you could think of questions that you might have about this work," Raz said. "About what this work means for those of us who are no longer acrobats, and what the work means for audiences."

On that note, Xiaohong walked to the line of acrobats and held up a paper. A paper with a particular phrase in Mandarin that was a favorite of Lu Yi's. One that harkened back to the early Youth Circus days, when the students yelled it together to mark the beginning of class: "Qín xué kǔ liàn!" meaning, to study and train diligently. This phrase and another one—"xièxie nǐ," which is "thank you"—served as bookends for the two-hour weekday classes at the Youth Circus. Sometimes the first one got lost in the shuffle as folks rolled in late or got distracted while changing clothes. But the "xièxie nǐ" at the end stayed remarkably consistent through the years. For the students, it meant more than a simple "thank you" for teaching. Ron Oppenheimer thought of it this way: "It's 'thank you to me, and thank you to you, and your family for putting in the work to be here.' So, grateful for the opportunity, in all aspects of the word grateful."

Those twin feelings of gratefulness and respect flew around the gym that day, as much as the flips, hops, twists, tucks, and occasional falling hoops. Much of the audience was made up of Lu Yi's former students, youth and adult students alike, or parents of former students. The youngest attendees—toddlers and babies, that is—carried with them the possibility of joining the next generation of acrobatic students at the Circus Center, who will inherit the methods and techniques passed down by Lu Yi, Xia Ke Min, and Xiaohong. This mélange of appreciation, finality, and continuity was clear to those present, from the acrobats to the crowd.

"There was, like, this interesting sense of awe from a lot of the adults who are parents of kids in the Youth Circus, and other adults who had heard about the Youth Circus," Dominic Cruz said. "There was a sense of, 'Wow, this is a very interesting thing. It is a privilege to see this.'"

Cruz, as of this writing a cast member of *Dear San Francisco*, took the opportunity to test some old skills, despite a six-month break from acrobatic practice. "I tried to bust a full twist through four hoops and I hit the first one," Cruz said, meaning he accidentally hit the hoop, knocking it to the ground. "I looked over at Mr. Lu Yi, and he just kind of furrowed his brow a little bit." Cruz managed to land the trick soon after, and he did get some pointers from Lu Yi: "He said, 'Good, good.' But to make sure I have stronger ankles, and have a better donkey kick, to push more with my arms."

Overall, though, Lu Yi stayed fairly quiet that day. Xiaohong pushed his wheelchair to the center for the lineup, then pushed him back to the side as the students made their rows for kicks. Xiaohong ran the class through their drills, ferrying back and forth from the mats to confer with Lu Yi, as old friends, former students, and well-wishers tried to take advantage of a now-rare public appearance to say hello. Judy Finelli sat next to Lu Yi, giving her a chance to reminisce.

"I was the 'culprit' who brought him here," Finelli said, referring to her 1989-90 push to convince Lu Yi to leave China, work with the Pickles, and join the circus school. Finelli recalled the U.S. immigration process, and remembered listing Lu Yi as "a distinguished artist of merit" on the paperwork signifying that there was no one in America who could teach what he knew.

"I recognized that without the Chinese training, without question America would never become competitive enough on the world stage to get anywhere," Finelli said. "Everybody would learn as I did, from performers here and there. I did pretty well, but thought there was a better way."

That better way ran through Lu Yi, who, as we know, accepted the offer—eventually.

"And I guess the rest is American acrobatic history," Finelli said.

True enough. But for the person at the center of the day, thinking of his career as history would be out of character. The masterclass carried a tinge of bittersweet feelings for Lu Yi.

"I was very proud and happy to be there, but at the same time very anxious," Lu Yi said later, with his daughter Lu Yue translating. "I wish I could do more."

Lu Yi would have preferred to be up and about, teaching the masterclass. He would have preferred to teach that next generation of acrobats, the ones squirming around in the bleachers, too. It's a sentiment most dedicated artists can relate to: watching the thing you love most from the side, grateful to be there but wishing you could jump in like you did before age, injury, work, life, or whatever got in the way. For Lu Yi, it was health concerns that prevented him from coaching yet another generation in the art of Chinese Acrobatics. Thankfully, those health concerns did not prevent him from seeing that his life's work would continue. That his students and other acrobats from around the world would carry on the tradition, here in San Francisco and elsewhere. He watched those folks line up one last time, in height order, to thank him for the lessons on acrobatics, and the lessons on the importance of learning diligently.

We say it all together, after a one-two-three: "Xièxie nǐ!"

AFTERWORD:
LEARNING HOW TO LEARN

BY DEVIN HOLT

I first met Master Trainer Lu Yi through a magazine profile. This was in 2001, when I saw the circus magazine *Spectacle* on a table in the San Francisco School of Circus Arts, where I had recently started training. The school, with its openness to teaching all levels of uninitiated circus dreamers (a crucial selling point) and connections to the radical theater and hippie ethos of the 1960s, had seemed like the perfect excuse to end my vagabond lifestyle and move to San Francisco. I figured I would fit in great—until I read that magazine profile. The article, written by Harriet Heyman, offered a fascinating look at the life, training history, and acrobatic philosophy of the school's artistic director. Reading about Lu Yi left me impressed, but even more so, intimidated.

Here was someone who had spent his life working in the world of true circus professionals; and who had invented a number of famed acrobatic tricks, despite facing physical abuse and government repression. I, by contrast, was an early twenties wannabe. A street corner hippie kid who twirled devil sticks at psychedelic rock shows and learned to juggle three balls at a Rainbow Gathering in Oregon, then tried to turn it into a career largely because I didn't know what else to do with myself.

Why, I thought, *would an important, influential, award-winning acrobatics trainer like Lu Yi want to work with someone like me?*

It seemed impossible. Lu Yi sounded more like someone I would find at one of the Canadian or European circus schools, the places so good I didn't even bother to audition. But, soon enough, I discovered the answer to my question. It was surprisingly obvious: Lu Yi loved circus arts. If you loved circus arts too, he was happy to share his knowledge.

I was not alone in carrying a nervous reverence for the school's famous coach. During one of my first classes there—called Circus 101—the instructor, Xiaohong Weng, paused to stare when Lu Yi happened to walk past the room. Lu Yi didn't come in, but he may have glanced toward us through the small window in the red, wooden door.

"That's my boss," Xiaohong said. His words slipped out in a reverent half-whisper. "Lu Yi. Very famous in China."

The class, a mix of recreational and aspirational students, craned our necks toward the window but could only glimpse the side profile of an older Chinese man walking slowly through the hall, probably heading to the main gym. He had short black hair and wore thin-framed glasses and a light, simple sweater. His gaze was aimed toward the floor. Soon after, he passed by again on his way out the main entrance. Lu Yi was headed home to Berkeley, after a day of teaching that started around nine or ten in the morning. It was almost eight o'clock at night.

Xiaohong did not take that brief appearance by his boss as a chance to indulge our curiosity. Instead, he pushed us more. We quickly returned to Circus 101—handstands on the wall; cartwheels, shoulder rolls, and dive rolls; deep, painful stretches; rola bola practice; three-ball juggling, etc. In retrospect, I'm not surprised by Xiaohong's reaction. He had worked with Lu Yi in a completely different setting from this welcoming, Americanized circus school. He knew how seriously Lu Yi took training, even for beginners.

"He was like a scary person—a big boss—in China," Xiaohong told me years later, when I approached him about this book project.

But, here in the United States, Lu Yi embraced a more friendly approach, one that Xiaohong noticed in 1994, after Lu Yi arranged a performance contract for him with Princess Cruises: "I saw him again, it was totally different—the feeling—the person I know from China." Lu Yi even thanked Xiaohong for taking the contract. "I was like, 'Whoa, is that the same person I know?'"

I started training with Lu Yi a year or so after that first class, and eventually became familiar with both aspects of his personality. Lu Yi was often warm and friendly, especially outside of class, and he liked to crack jokes. He once quipped that the number of people who were clapping when I played a Phish live album in the gym was "impressive." (The band is famously noisy, and a bit of an acquired taste.) However, Lu Yi could get quite grumpy during training. Once, in an attempt to demonstrate the amount of tension that should be in my leg, he slapped my calf hard enough to leave a bruise. If you made the same mistake enough times, Lu Yi might give a long, disappointed, "Noooo. Not good. Too loose, just flopping everywhere."

Unlike some high-level coaches, Lu Yi never looked down

on people who only trained in acrobatics for fun and exercise, as so many of the adult students did. But if you wanted to be a performer, Lu Yi expected more. You had to train more. You had to stretch more. Above all, you had to learn the handstand. And none of this came easily. Training in acrobatics can be terrible. It hurts. Sometimes you get injured. Sometimes you work on the same thing all day and never get it right. Sometimes you want to eat junk food and stay out late instead of eating right and training early. Lu Yi said it best: "Training is bitter." Some days, Lu Yi would cross his arms, shake his head, and add: "Very bitter."

When it came time to launch my performance career, I veered back into my own lane: juggling, dance, and humor. The tricks I learned from Lu Yi never really made it into my acts, aside from the occasional cartwheel or dive roll. After two and a half years of hard training, it was obvious that I had either started too late or didn't possess the talent to be a serious acrobat. My handstands were pretty good, by U.S. standards, but my tumbling was awful. Still, I learned a lot more than tricks from my training with Lu Yi.

I learned about focus, discipline, and the sacrifices behind creative work—the sweat and toil you see in movie montages. I learned about the importance of basics. I learned that you have to build the foundation before you paint the house. I learned, essentially, how to learn from Lu Yi. Those lessons stayed with me through ten years of performances; through jobs in event management and marketing; and through a second round of schooling when I got my master's at the CUNY Graduate School of Journalism in New York City. My circus background played a big part in my admittance to the school and my selection for four journalism internships. (One editor flat-out told me I got picked because I was "in the circus.")

When Lu Yi semi-retired in 2014, I was not paying much attention to circus, focusing purely on learning how to write and preparing for graduate school. But I knew his story deserved a fresh telling, one I started thinking about more seriously in January of 2017, about a month after graduation.

To be sure, this book and Heyman's excellent 2001 profile in *Spectacle* magazine are not the only pieces of media on Lu Yi's life. He's what my journalism professors might have called a five-year profile—someone prominent or interesting who is worth profiling every five years. Circus magazines and San Francisco's news organizations have treated him as such, and, for the visually inclined, there is the documentary *Bizarre: A Circus Story*, produced by Weird Pixel and directed by Meg Pinsonneault (highly recommended).

This book could have been done as a standard biography, and I would have read that version for sure. What I really wanted, though, was for people to have an understanding of the Lu Yi I knew: the person who changed circus in China and in the U.S., the master trainer who taught his students about acrobatics and life. And I wanted Lu Yi to tell his own story. My role has been that of a compiler, arranger, and transcriber.

We approached the process with mixed methods. At first, I visited Lu Yi alone. I later hired a translator, Laura Fanelli, for some of the early sessions. Eventually, Lu Yi convinced his daughter Lu Yue to be the main translator. The three of us kept a standing Saturday afternoon conference call appointment during those strange, stay-at-home months of 2020. We hardly ever talked about the news, politics, or the pandemic. Only about circus, and the occasional mention of old friends.

Some days, I asked good questions that led to interesting anecdotes. On other days, I asked poor questions that led to one-word answers. Sometimes, Lu Yi felt talkative and the memories flowed. Other times, they were too far away, or too painful, to talk about. I also did a lot of reading about China and Chinese Acrobatics; I interviewed Lu Yi's friends, colleagues, and students; and I pored over all the aforementioned years of media on Lu Yi. The research and interviews aided the narrative and served as the basis for the third-person chapters sprinkled throughout the book. For Chinese names, which use a different naming convention than American English, I used the name the person was best-known by in the United States. In the memoir sections, if Lu Yi's recollection of an event differed from that of his friends or colleagues, I went with Lu Yi's version. This is his story, after all.

As with any book of this nature (and as mentioned in the opening disclaimer), the recreated scenes, dialogue, and anecdotes are subject to the fallible nature of memory and the challenges of translation. Unique to this particular book, they are also subject to my limited talent. For that much, I apologize.

Regardless, I hope you enjoyed reading Lu Yi's story even half as much as I enjoyed hearing it.

ACKNOWLEDGMENTS

Every book is an ensemble, and this one is no exception. If *Training is Bitter* made a playbill, it would look something like this:

Master Trainer: Lu Yi

Word Compiler: Devin Holt

Translators: Lu Yue, Laura Fanelli

Developmental and Copy Editor: Zhui Ning Chang

Design: Domini Dragoone

Photos: Terry Lorant, Nanjing Acrobatic Troupe

Youth Circus Alums: Dominic Cruz, Maya Kesselman Cruz, Joren Dawson, Devin Henderson, Or Oppenheimer, Ron Oppenheimer

Beta Readers: Jeff Raz, Genie Cartier, Dian Meechai, Xiaohong Weng

Special thanks for memories, guidance, clarifications, phone calls, photo searches, reading suggestions, ideas, gripes, random thoughts and general helpfulness to: Lu Na, Wang Hong Zhu, Xia Ke Min, Judy Finelli, Pete Jacobson, Ayla Bell, Diane Wasnak, Dominique Jando, Leslie Tipton, Felicity Hesed, Adriana Baer, Virginia Hubbell, Paul Binder, Lorenzo Pisoni, Will Underwood, Karen Quest, Christina Weiland, Jillian Ashley, Stanley Wang, Lin Quing, Seth Golub, JooWan Kim, Shawn Rose, Will Underwood, and Gary Thomsen.

ABOUT DEVIN HOLT

Devin Holt has been a lot of things: A wayward street-corner youth, a circus performer, and a farm boy loading firewood into the family pick up truck. He has hitchhiked across the United States more than once; lived in the rafters of a communal artist warehouse in San Francisco; and studied kung fu in a quiet academy on top of a hill in rural China. Now, he writes.

Printed in Great Britain
by Amazon

38569797R00108